COSCOM ENTERTAINMENT

THE WRAITH
Eyes of Judgment

The Official

Script Book
&
Movie Guide

COSCOM ENTERTAINMENT
WINNIPEG

Coscom Entertainment
Suite 2, 317 Edison Ave.
Winnipeg, MB R2G 0L9

This book is a work of fiction. Names, characters, places and events either are products of the author's imagination or are used fictitiously. Any resemblance to actual events or persons living or dead is purely coincidental. All characters are the intellectual property of Frank Dirscherl and are based on the Trinity Comic of the same name. The opinions and views expressed in the interviews contained within as those of the individuals and do not necessarily reflects the opinions and views of Coscom Entertainment.

ISBN 1-897217-12-9

The Wraith: Eyes of Judgment – The Official Script Book & Movie Guide

Published by Coscom Entertainment
www.coscomentertainment.com

For more on The Wraith, please visit www.the-wraith.com
For more on Sir Reel Films, please visit www.sir-reelfilms.com

Front Cover Photo by Best Friends Photos
Back Cover Poster by Iskandar Salim
Interior Photos by Best Friends Photos
Cover Layout and Design by A.P. Fuchs
End of book comic preview art by Eliseu Gouveia, Mitch Ballard, Jim Taylor and Jeff Austin

Library and Archives Canada Cataloguing in Publication

Dirscherl, Frank, 1973-
The wraith : eyes of judgment : script book & movie guide / Frank Dirscherl, Stephen Semones.

ISBN 1-897217-12-9

I. Semones, Stephen, 1977- II. Title.

PN1997.W722D57 2005 791.43'72 C2005-904734-8

Printed and bound in the USA

To my dearest Lisa, for her love and inspiration;
and my family, as always.

- Frank Dirscherl

For Sean.
This one's for you.
And to Pauline,
for your inspiration, kindness, and
most of all, your love. I miss you.

- Stephen Semones

Contents

THE WRAITH
Eyes of Judgment

Written by

Stephen J. Semones & Frank Dirscherl

Based on The Wraith

created by
Frank Dirscherl

and published by
Trinity Comics

OPENING CREDITS AND EPIC LARRY GROUPÉ MUSIC

FADE IN:

CGI SEQUENCE

EXT. CITY SKYLINE - NIGHT

A city of towering darkness and fear, intimidation and creeping shadows, a city of corruption and vice. This is Metro City!

TITLE: Metro City

END CGI SEQUENCE

EXT. ROOFTOP - NIGHT

We see a CLOAKED FIGURE perched on a rooftop looking down into an alley. Shadows surrounding the figure limit a clear view, but it's apparent that he's seeking out criminal prey... (possibly some greenscreen stuff here?)

With one quick maneuver, the figure flings it's shroud around and disappears over the edge of the roof and into the darkness of the alley below.

CUT TO:

EXT. ALLEY - NIGHT

Two common criminals or hired thugs run down an alley. They each wear the stereotypical ski masks and brandish pistols. One of the men, MIKEY is carrying a small bag, apparently filled with cash. The other man and brains of the operation, OTTO, searches the alley for an escape.

OTTO

This way!

He points down the alley and they both round a corner.

MIKEY

I don't know, I think we've already been this way!

OTTO
Shut up, I know where we're going.

They get to the end of the alley and stop. Dead end. Otto sizes up the situation and turns to Mikey. He points to Mikey's left.

OTTO (cont.)
Quick, try to open that door!

Mikey shakes and twists the doorknob to no avail. Otto, getting frustrated, pushes Mikey to the side.

OTTO (cont.)
You gotta have muscle to pry it open! Idiot!

Mikey, ashamed at his failure, starts to wonder off to "look out". He gets halfway up the alley and stops suddenly.

MIKEY
Good God!

He drops to his knees in fear.

OTTO
(still trying to open the door)
Will you shut up and look out for the cops?

Mikey is paralyzed with fear. He lifts the mask over his face and stares at the presence in front of him.

Suddenly two glowing, yellow eyes pierce the darkness - the eyes of judgment! They come close to Mikey and he starts to cry.

Otto, becoming totally upset with Mikey, turns around almost in a yell.

OTTO (cont.)
I said shut the He... Oh my God! What is that thing?

Suddenly, Mikey is thrown back down the alley landing on top of Otto. Both men, trying to regain their composure, cannot say a word, but somehow feel 'drawn' to the eyes. Otto, getting back his bearings, draws his pistol and aims at the eyes.

OTTO (cont.)
Say goodnight freak!

A dark blue, gloved hand reaches out and strips him of his gun, breaking his wrist in the process. The gun drops to the ground and out of sight. Otto screams in pain. Mikey is still staring into the eyes when suddenly the same hand grabs him by the throat and lifts him high into the air.

Mikey is thrown like a rag doll into the door he tried to open only moments ago. He falls to the cold pavement in silence.

Otto lunges for the figure, but finds himself caught by the throat mid-air.

OTTO (cont.)
Son of a bi...

The grasp gets tight and stops Otto from speaking. The figure starts to speak, as Otto's eyes grow wild with panic, fear, and rage. The figure releases its grip allowing Otto to cough and catch his breath.

OTTO (cont.)
(gasping)
You have no idea who you're dealing with. When my boss finds out...

FIGURE
I know who your boss is. Tell him that his sins will find him out.

Otto is thrown high into the air dropping down on top of Mikey, who is starting to come to.

Mikey looks up as the yellow eyes drift back into the darkness. The figure speaks again.

FIGURE (cont.)
Justice is coming! Tell your boss that I'm coming for him.

Mikey starts to whimper as he sees the unconscious body of Otto pinning him to the ground. He looks down the alley in complete and total fear with tears streaming down his face.

He buries his face in his hands as we...

CUT TO: BLACK

FADE INTO:

INT. BEDROOM - MORNING

A digital clock strikes 6:50 and the radio alarm comes on. The radio clicks on halfway through a newscast.

REPORTER
...Still nothing is known about the events surrounding the apprehension of the two dangerously, armed robbers of Metro Jewelers. Police Commissioner Harrison was unavailable for comment.

We see a man roll over in bed and stare at the clock. He seems to be listening intently to the newscast.

REPORTER (cont.)
Reports of a masked vigilante flooded the newsroom again early this morning. The sightings of a man dressed with a cape and two glowing yellow eyes on his chest have been a regular occurrence in Metro City this year, but as usual, we have been unable to gain any confirmation from City Hall. We have continued our own investigations, but as yet, we have been unable to obtain any conclusive proof. Commissioner Harrison stated last week at a press conference that if such a vigilante exists, he or she is in fact no way related to the precinct, and will be arrested and prosecuted if caught.

The man in bed chuckles at the report. He continues to listen intently for some groundbreaking news.

REPORTER (cont.)
The toll of captured criminals rumored due to this mysterious vigilante now stands at an impressive twenty-seven. Stay tuned to WMTC 98.5 for more details on the hour, every hour. This is...

CLICK. The radio is switched off as we see the man sit up on the edge of the bed. He rubs his eyes and turns his head back to see his beautiful girlfriend still fast asleep.

The man, MICHAEL REEVE, starts to get dressed for another day at the "office". His girlfriend, LEENA PATTERSON, stirs briefly before wishing the man in her life the best of luck.

LEENA
Looking forward to the new assignment handsome?

MICHAEL
Not really. This masked vigilante guy has got everyone at the station in a bind. I guess I never should have put my name on that questionnaire. It's my own fault that I've been put out to do some lousy surveillance and undercover job.

LEENA
You'll do great as always. Look, you're a good man, and if no other cop you call a partner can see it, I can, and that's all that matters. Right?

Michael, putting his holstered gun under his shirt, smiles, leans over and kisses her gently on the cheek.

MICHAEL
So, you have a big day planned?

LEENA
The new shipment of books arrive this morning, so Tech Services will be busy cataloging those for the better half of the day. We're so short staffed; even the Reference team is involved...

MICHAEL
Sounds exciting.

Michael peeks out the window, almost contemplating not going into work.

LEENA
It'll be fine. You'll see. When all the red tape surrounding this vigilante clears, and they catch the guy, you'll be back with a partner in no time.

Michael starts to leave, but not before turning to blow a kiss to Leena.

LEENA (cont.)
Love ya!

MICHAEL
You too!

Leena smiles as Michael leaves. She then turns back over and looks at the clock. It reads 6:56.

LEENA
How does he get up this early?

CUT TO:

EXT. HOTEL - DAY

We see a well-dressed man with long, black hair walk up a hotel sidewalk. He carries only a small clothes bag and a metal briefcase.

INT. HOTEL - DAY

The man walks to the counter and pulls out a credit card.

MAN
Single room.

The receptionist takes the card and looks him over.

RECEPTIONIST
How long will you be staying sir?

The receptionist slides him a piece of paper and a pen. He signs the paper and takes back his credit card.

MAN
Indefinitely.

He is handed a swipe card/key and casually walks away. The receptionist gives him an odd glance and then goes back to work.

The man walks across the lobby and to an elevator.

CUT TO:

INT. HOTEL ROOM - DAY

We see the same man now sitting at the room's desk. His briefcase sits directly in front of him. He is about to open it when his pager goes off. Giving him a slight startle, he checks the number.

He pulls out his cell phone and dials the number. He pauses for a moment as he listens for an answer. He eyes the briefcase the whole time.

MAN
Yes?
(a beat)
He wants to drop the funding? But the expedition has been already fully planned!
(a beat)
It's too late to pull out now!

His eyes grow intense with anger. He begins to breathe harder as he continues to stare at the case.

MAN (cont.)
Do you even know who I am?

The answer to his question infuriates him, and while he holds his fury in check, his words have a bite to them.

MAN (cont.)
You tell Latham that he still owes me. True power is in our grasp, and I won't let anyone stop me now!!

He throws his phone down in a rage. He sits back in his chair and begins to calm. He smiles, and opens the case. He pulls forth an object wrapped in cloth.

MAN (cont.)
I'm so close now. Latham can't stop me. Nobody can.
(a beat, ominous)
Nobody...

He begins to unravel the cloth as we...

CUT TO:

EXT. METRO CITY STREETS - DAY

Michael Reeve walks down a street and into an alley. The same alley The Wraith was seen in the night before. As he walks through the alley looking around, he hears someone behind him. He turns to see a shadowy figure standing at the end of the alley.

MICHAEL
Excuse me, I'd like to ask you a few questions.

The figure steps closer and what appears to be a vagrant steps into the light.

DUTCH
Whatya want?

MICHAEL
Name to start with.

DUTCH
Name's Dutch, and I live here. You're standing in my living room.

He laughs mockingly.

MICHAEL
I'm sorry, but I'm conducting an official police investigation...

DUTCH
Bullshit! The 'real' cops was here this mornin'. What the Hell you doin' here?

MICHAEL
Just what I said.

Dutch clearly doesn't believe him.

MICHAEL (cont.)
Okay then, why don't <u>you</u> tell me what I'm doing here?

DUTCH
You're lookin' for that Wraith aint'cha?

MICHAEL
Why would you?? ...Have you seen him?

DUTCH
Hell yeah I seen 'em. Kicked the shit outta two punks last night. Beat the Hell outta 'em, and then left 'em for the po'lice.

MICHAEL
What did he look like? After the incident, did you see which way he headed?

DUTCH
He wore himself a cape and hood. Had two big 'ol yeller eyes on his chest. Didn't see where he went off to, but it was in a hurry.

MICHAEL
How do I know you're telling me the truth, and you're not some drunken bum?

DUTCH
'Cause he left this behind.

Dutch sticks out his dirty hand to reveal THE WRAITH'S MASK. Michael snatches it away and looks at it as if it's a priceless artifact.

MICHAEL
Where did you get this?

DUTCH
He took it off down the way there. I came out of my corner to see what all the commotion was 'bout, and he saw me and ran. I picked that up and hung on to it, thinking he'd be back for it, but he never came.

MICHAEL
Thanks.

Michael takes off with the mask in a hurry, exiting the alley. Dutch looks after him angrily.

DUTCH
Hey ya bastard! That's mine!

CUT TO:

INT. HOTEL ROOM - EVENING

The man still sits at the desk. In front of him lie very old pieces of parchment with ancient runes and archaic symbols written on them.

He is now wearing glasses and reading over the very old papers closely. Suddenly, he rises up and smiles. He looks over to the bed.

Resting on the bed is a scepter of sorts. A small and very old artifact that appears of African origin. It shines in the low light. A truly priceless artifact it is.

FADE OUT TO:

INT. MICHAEL'S APARTMENT - NIGHT

Michael sits at his desk, talking on the phone to Leena. He's holding the mask up to the light studying it as he talks to her.

MICHAEL
...I don't know why he'd leave it.
Unless...

He looks at it closer.

MICHAEL (cont.)
He was leaving this for me to find.
Leena, I know this sounds crazy, but
I think he almost knew I'd be there
this morning.
(pause)
Ok, I promise I'll get some rest. See
you tomorrow for lunch?

He cannot take his eyes off of it.

MICHAEL (cont.)
Love you too. Goodnight.

As soon as he puts the phone on the receiver, a loud knock suddenly rings out from his door.

MICHAEL (cont.)
Who the hell could that be at
this hour?

He shoves the mask into a drawer and leaps from his chair.

He opens the door and sees nothing. Turning from the door he starts back inside when someone falls down behind him on his patio. Turning back, he sees a shadowy figure kneeling down in front of him, through the open patio door.

MICHAEL (cont.)
It's you. It's really you... I have
so many questions...

We don't see with whom Michael is speaking, but we can assume who it is.

MICHAEL (cont.)
I've got your mask inside. Let me get it for you...

Suddenly Michael sees what is wrong.

MICHAEL (cont.)
You're... wounded! Oh my God! You need help...

Michael is suddenly cut off by a low and gurgling voice.

THE WRAITH
You're the one, Michael Reeve. You are the one.

Michael looks on with a mixture of awe and terror on his face.

Two gloved hands reach for Michael's head, grasping each side at the temples. A BRIGHT FLASH occurs as we...

QUICK CUT TO:

INT. HOTEL ROOM - NIGHT

The man holds the artifact in one hand and uses his other hand to skim over the paper.

MAN
Sil kael baba wey...

He continues scanning the papers, trying to interpret the language. A low fog begins to encircle him. He doesn't seem to notice it slowly drifting across the floor toward him.

MAN (cont.)
Ver ada cohn... sue wey sil...

His fingers come across a symbol resembling a cobra. He looks at the artifact and back to the papers.

CGI SEQUENCE

The artifact begins to glow green. The man tries to put it down but can't. He sits back in his chair from the force of the glow. It is physically pushing him down.

He tenses up; absorbing whatever forces this scepter is putting out. His face screams in horror, but only silently. It's as if he cannot hardly move or speak at all. He starts to bleed just above his right eye. Blood trickles down his face, covering his eye.
END CGI

Suddenly he stops moving in the chair. The force behind the scepter stops, leaving him unconscious. It drops from his hand and onto the floor.

Blood covers most of the right side of his face. His head slumps forward as we...

FADE INTO:

INT. LEENA'S APARTMENT - DAY

TITLE: One Week Later

Leena enters her apartment rapidly and sits down on the couch. Pulling her oval-shaped glasses off, she rubs her eyes. She's cried herself out.

Putting her glasses back on, she reaches for the answering machine and hits the play button.

The tape winds itself to the appropriate place and stops suddenly.

A female's voice familiar to her starts to speak on the recording.

ASTRID (VO)
Leena, it's Astrid. Look, why not take the rest of the week off at least. I really don't think work is the best place for you right now. After seeing you break down and cry yesterday, I really think the best place for you right now is home. Everything will work out for the best, I promise. Talk to you soon, dear.

Leena smiles tearfully as she hits the erase button. The next message starts as a man's deep voice crackles over the small speaker.

SLOAN (VO)
Miss Patterson? Detective Bob Sloan here, we spoke about a week ago at Michael's place. I wanted you to know that the blood that was in his apartment... came back as a perfect match... it's Michael's.

Leena listens intently, almost bursting into tears at the news.

SLOAN (VO, cont.)
Look, I know not everyone on the force agreed with Michael, but I counted him as a friend. I'm doing everything in my power to see the sum-bitches responsible brought to justice.
(pause)
Look, you were the last person to see or talk with him, that's pretty much all we have to go on right now. If you remember anything important, anything, you call me! My home number is five...

CLICK. The machine cut him off mid-sentence. She hits erase on the machine once more. The next message starts to play.

MOTHER (VO)
Leena, it's your mother dear. Call me back as soon as possible. I need to know you're okay. Oh, this silly machine! Is this thing recording? Call me back, dear.

She hits erase once more and sits back on the couch. She pulls her glasses off once more, but this time starts to cry.

CUT TO:

INT. DARK ROOM - EVENING

A man sits alone in a dark room facing a window. The lights from the outside create a brooding atmosphere, giving the room an impending evil look. He smokes an expensive Cuban cigar with casual charm, as he looks out to the night sky.

The man stands, continues looking out the window. This is ROBERT LATHAM, head of Latham Industries, a conglomerate with interests as diverse as electronics and fossil fuels. What most don't know, however, is that Latham is also the head of the largest crime cartel on the eastern seaboard. A second man, his deputy CHARLIE GRIECO walks up behind him, saying nothing at first, but soon speaks up.

GRIECO
Mr Latham... sir?
(pause)
The Afghans are ready to deal.

The man at the window turns around. Shadows still engulf his whole body. We see an evil silhouette showing Latham within the darkness.

LATHAM
They can wait.

He puffs on his cigar.

GRIECO
We can't keep them waiting long.

Latham looks at Grieco briefly, mildly annoyed, before...

FLASH CUT TO:

A black and white shot of THE WRAITH and Grieco standing face to face. Grieco smiles and steps backward.

BACK TO:

LATHAM
They can wait a little longer. Let me savor my triumph.

FLASH CUT TO:

Another black and white image flash of The Wraith hitting the floor, after being shot in the chest, in what appears to be a shipyard warehouse. Blood covers the floor where he hits.

BACK TO:

GRIECO
The Wraith? You think you nailed him this time?

Latham says nothing, again looking at Grieco as though mildly annoyed.

GRIECO (cont.)
We thought so before and failed. Are you sure he's out of the picture now?

Leaning forward from the shadows, we now get a vivid glimpse of the multi-millionaire and crime lord. His aging face appears devilish in the darkened room.

LATHAM
No-one could survive what I put him through. I saw that bullet pierce his heart. No matter what else he is, The Wraith is still human.

FLASH CUT TO:

Another black and white shot of The Wraith crawling, marking a trail of blood behind him as he moves along.

BACK TO:

GRIECO
I suggest we keep a close eye on this shipment. Those Afghans are getting impatient, and I don't want anyone screwing things up, especially The Wraith!

Latham looks a little angrier, but keeps it under control.

LATHAM
(angry)
The Wraith is dead!
(pause, calms)
Everything is being handled with the greatest care, Charlie. I'm handling this personally, so... you can get back to your duties now!

Grieco looks a combination of chagrined and defiant. He has power aspirations, but knows the time is not yet right.

GRIECO
Something's not right, I'm telling you, I can feel it.

Latham stands.

LATHAM
I'm handling this, Charlie, that's all you need concern yourself with.

Latham takes his seat once more, and leans back, triumphant in the knowledge that he's beaten The Wraith... or so he thinks. He spins the chair around to the window as smoke billows up from the seat. Grieco exits sullenly, mumbling to himself under his breath... his time will come.

CUT TO:

INT. HOTEL ROOM - NIGHT

The strange man stands before the mirror in the bathroom of his hotel room. He stares menacingly as his reflection casts back sheer horror. His right eye is solid white now - no pupil. Around the same eye, a Cobra has been scarred into his skin.

He begins to smile fiendishly. His new appearance is very intimidating.

MAN
(harsh, grating voice)
Latham... I'm coming for you...
(pauses)

The expedition would have yielded us both unlimited power. The scepter alone has given me...

He stops himself, turns, shifts back into the main area of the hotel room.

MAN (cont.)
What do I care for the expedition now. I have power beyond reason!
(a beat)
This city will bow to me as its conqueror! I'm coming for you, Latham...

His face contorts back into a solemn stare. His face shows signs of disdain and pity all at once. A true madman he has become, though to what extent his power and madness extend, we don't know.

MAN (cont.)
... the Cobra is coming!

INT. LEENA'S APARTMENT - NIGHT

Leena lies in bed fast asleep. A solemn expression rests on her face as she sleeps. Her face almost shows no signs of dreams.

As she sleeps, a hand comes into view and gently touches her cheek.

LEENA
(whispers)
Michael... ?

Her eyes open and she looks up in surprise.

CAMERA PULLS BACK

She's alone. A dream of her lost love just haunted her thoughts. However, the look on her face is almost enough to know that Michael is still alive. Somewhere.

She rises from the bed and walks into her bathroom. Hearing the typical flush of a toilet and water running, she stays in the bathroom shaking off the dream by splashing water across her face.

Exiting the bathroom, she climbs back into the bed, glancing over at a picture of her and Michael. She smiles.

LEENA (cont.)
There has to be more to this...

She drops her head back on the pillow and closes her eyes. As she turns on her side to go back to sleep, she starts to think out loud.

LEENA (cont.)
I know you're out there Michael. I can feel you.

CAMERA PANS UP

As she lies in bed we see the window above her and a silhouetted figure looking in on her. We see The Wraith looking down on her as we focus through the darkness.

FADE OUT:

EXT. LEENA'S APARTMENT - NIGHT

The Wraith moves from the window and walks down the fire escape gracefully. He leaps at the bottom landing in almost a perfect ballet landing. His cape surrounds him as he crouches with the landing.

He darts into a nearby alley as we...

CUT TO:

EXT. ROOFTOP - NIGHT

The Wraith is perched atop a building looking down on Metro City's nightlife. His face is lined with a curious look as he peers down like a marble gargoyle.

The Wraith reacts as if someone's talking to him. He pushes his mask at the temple.

THE WRAITH
I'm here.

We here a thick Irish accent coming from his ear radio; the voice: MAX HORTON, The Wraith's driver and mechanic.

MAX (VO)
Chief, we got nothing on the police scanner. Seems quiet tonight.

THE WRAITH
I'll continue my patrol. Keep listening for anything out of the ordinary.

He pushes at his temple again, clicking the radio off with an audible CLICK. He rests his chin in his hands and looks out onto the city. He begins to think out loud.

THE WRAITH (cont.)
She seems so familiar. Why do I feel so drawn to her? What does she have to do with...

A scream pierces the night from below him, a woman screaming out in terror. Alert, he forgets his moment of self-questioning and leaps from the ledge.

CUT TO:

EXT. ALLEY - NIGHT

Two men, CHAINS and SQUIRE, hold a WOMAN by each arm. Their buddy, EIGHT BALL walks slowly toward her, brandishing a knife and smiling widely. She is in sheer terror and trying to free herself to no avail.

EIGHT BALL
Let's see what you got under that dress.

He holds the knife to her throat, daring her to scream. CHAINS and SQUIRE still clutch her arms like two sentinels.

WOMAN
Please, I'll give you all the money I have. Please, just let me go.

CHAINS
Shut up!

Chains smacks her across the mouth sending her down to the cold, wet pavement. SQUIRE picks her back up by her hair and forces her arms behind her back.

EIGHT BALL
No chance lady. We want more than money. We want a little piece of the pie.

He gives an evil laugh and grabs her chin forcing her to look at him.

A shadow forms behind them in the darkness. SQUIRE catches a glimpse and motions to CHAINS.

SQUIRE
We got company!

CHAINS
(to the woman)
When we're done with him, we'll come back to you. Don't move!

Squire forces the woman into Eight Ball's arms and he immediately turns to face the shadow with the knife to her neck.

EIGHT BALL
Any closer and the girl gets a second smile.

He motions the knife across her neck in a cutting motion. Chains and Squire enter the darkness.

Suddenly we hear Squire squeal in pain as he flies backward out of the dark alleyway and lands unconscious at Eight Ball's feet. Eight Ball looks on curiously as two figures emerge from the darkness.

Chains stumbles forward into the light with a gloved hand gripping him by his hair. Following Chains, The Wraith steps forward directly behind him. He throws Chains face first into the pavement. Chains doesn't move.

Eight Ball throws the woman against a nearby wall, sending her to her knees.

EIGHT BALL (cont.)

Son of a bitch, you just messed with the wrong man!

He lunges forward at The Wraith with the knife, aiming for his chest. With a lightning fast reflex, The Wraith sidesteps his attacker and grabs the knife from his grip. In the same moment, he spins around and grabs Eight Ball by the throat and forces him to look into the now glowing 'eyes of judgment' on his chest.

THE WRAITH

Feel the pain of those you have touched with your evil! Feel the shame and guilt that is rightfully yours!

The 'eyes' glow, crackling with an eerie energy, illuminating Eight Ball's face. Anguish sets in as he starts to cry and mumble incoherently.

He falls to the ground clutching his face and screaming in extreme mental anguish.

The Wraith walks to the fallen woman and extends a hand. Frightened, she nevertheless takes it, as he helps her up.

THE WRAITH (cont.)

Are you all right?

WOMAN

Yes... yes, I think so.

She turns around to grab her purse lying behind her. As she turns back around, The Wraith is gone. She looks all around and sees no one but her attackers lying unconscious.

WOMAN (cont.)

(whispers)

Thank you.

Shaken, she stumbles down the alley and into the darkness.

CUT TO:

INT. CAR - NIGHT

Max Horton sits at the wheel smoking a cigarette and listening to the radio. He looks in the rear-view mirror and sees The Wraith suddenly there in the backseat. He jumps slightly.

MAX

Damn!

THE WRAITH

Drive.

MAX

Where to now?

THE WRAITH

Just drive.

Max squeals the tires on the car as he pulls away from a darkened alley.

CUT TO:

INT. HOTEL ROOM - MORNING

We see the Cobra sitting by the window, curtains drawn tight. The light of the morning sun illuminates the drapes, casting him in dark, ominous shadows.

He is listening to a radio broadcast of the local news.

REPORTER

... And thanks again for listening to WMTC 98.5, your best news source for Metro City.

The Cobra sits, silent and motionless, listening to the broadcast.

REPORTER (cont.)

A local female resident of Metro City, whose name has yet to be disclosed, states the mysterious Wraith vigilante saved her from a brutal gang related attack. More details on this breaking story have yet to be obtained, but Police Commissioner Harrison has revealed that a press conference is set for next Monday.

(a beat)

In financial news, Robert Latham, Chief Executive of Latham Industries, announced today a record profit margin was achieved this financial...

CLICK! The Cobra switches off the radio, fury and madness etched in his sinister, terrifying features, as we...

FADE INTO:

EXT. LEENA'S APARTMENT - DAY

Leena, walking to her car, fumbles in her purse for her keys. As she approaches her car she looks up and sees what appears to be Michael across the street. He looks a little different, but it's still Michael. Startled, she starts to walk toward him curiously.

LEENA

Michael!

The man looks at her curiously and gets in the backseat of an adjacent car (piloted by Max). The car drives away leaving her standing in tears, utterly confused.

CUT TO:

INT. MICHAEL'S APARTMENT - DAY

The door bursts open and Leena walks in. There is no sign of anyone around. She walks, looking around for any clue to his disappearance. Was that really Michael she saw?

She walks to his desk and starts to look around. She opens a drawer and sees something that sparks her interest. Pulling out papers and notebooks, she removes a mask and holds it up to the light. Examining it, she looks it over intently.

Still clutching the mask, she walks into his bedroom. Lying on the bed, she continues to study the mask.

LEENA

(to herself)

I know you're not dead. I can feel it, and I can feel you. I won't leave here until you come back to me.

She gets up, throws the mask on the bed and walks out on the balcony.

EXT. MICHAEL'S BALCONY - DAY

Outside, she looks around curiously, but does not see the same man she saw earlier standing across the street looking up at her, hidden by the shadows in the alley below.
Casually she turns and walks back inside.

INT. MICHAEL'S APARTMENT - DAY

She walks to the bed and drops onto it. She grabs the mask again and looks over to a picture of her and Michael beside the bed.

A sudden and sharp knock on the door rouses her from her thoughts. She gets up and walks to the door, casually tossing the mask on a nearby desk.

She opens the door, but no one is there. She starts to close the door when she sees someone at the end of the hall rounding the corner.

LEENA

Hey!

INT. HALLWAY - DAY

She walks into the hall and toward the corner. She rounds it and spies a figure at the end of the corridor collapsed on the floor before the stairwell door. It looks like Michael.

LEENA

Michael?

She rushes to the person's side and quickly sees that it is indeed Michael, though he looks different, more built, more athletic, and his hair is in a different style.

She holds him in her arms and strokes his hair. He is out cold and cannot hear her.

LEENA (cont.)
Michael, what's wrong? Can you stand?

No answer. His eyes are rolled back in his head.

LEENA (cont.)
We have to get you to a hospital!

Suddenly, a familiar Irish voice is heard behind her.

MAX (VO)
Miss? I'll take it from here.

She turns around to see Max standing behind her looking at them with concern in his eyes. He extends a hand to help her up.

FADE OUT:

INT. LATHAM'S OFFICE - NIGHT

Darkness. We hear footsteps and suddenly a small light is switched on. We see Latham start walking toward his desk in the shadows.

THE COBRA (VO)
We need to talk, Robert.

Latham stops in his tracks just before he can reach the desk. He is taken off guard as he notices someone sitting in his chair. The chair is turned away from us, so he cannot see who is there.

LATHAM
(angry)
Who are you, how did you get in here?!

THE COBRA (VO)
Trust me Robert, we _do_ need to talk.

LATHAM
Turn and face me, you coward!

He remains silent, enraging Latham, who stands his ground.

LATHAM (cont.)
Who the hell are you?!

THE COBRA
Someone whose project you nurtured. Someone you strung along until it was too late. Someone you spurned!

The Cobra spins in his chair, facing Latham. Latham audibly gasps at the sight before him... this devilish man, his face scabbed over in a hideous wound in the shape of a Cobra around his right, marled eye. He smiles deviously at the crimelord. Latham, however, regains his cool quickly, and reaches down, grabs a cigar and lights it.

LATHAM
Do you know who you're dealing with here?

THE COBRA
Oh, I know exactly who and what you are, Robert.

Latham ambles from side-to-side in front of his own desk.

LATHAM
You've got guts, and talent to get in here undetected. You've got five minutes... what do you want?

THE COBRA
I'll take all the time I need, Robert and you are going to listen to every word.

LATHAM
Get on with it!

THE COBRA
Temper, Robert, temper.
(pause)
Here's the deal... I'm going to help

you and then you're going to help me.

LATHAM
How could you possibly help me?

The Cobra leans forward, his smile broadening.

THE COBRA
I'm going to kill The Wraith for you.

LATHAM
(mocks)
The Wraith's dead! You're a little behind the times, my friend.

The Cobra stands, his height and his menacing appearance, gives him a real edge.

THE COBRA
Dear, deluded Robert.
(pause)
He's alive. I can feel it. I know it! And I can rid you of him forever.

The Cobra smiles, and his marled eye gleams... his countenance so evil, so menacing, even Latham has a moment of concern.

CUT TO:

EXT. SANDERSON MANSION - NIGHT

Establishing shot of the grand home of multi-millionaire recluse Paul Sanderson.

INT. SANDERSON MANSION - NIGHT

Michael opens his eyes and spies Leena alongside him sitting on the edge of the bed. He makes a slight groan as he regains consciousness. He's still groggy.

LEENA
Michael, are you all right?

He grabs his head, tries to shake what appears to be a strong headache away.

MICHAEL
L... Leena... head hurts...

She holds his hands starts to stroke his hair.

LEENA
You've come back to me, I can't believe it. Thank God.

MICHAEL
Leena... I...

LEENA
I'm sorry Michael. I'm so sorry about everything.

Michael now appears fully awake, and the pain seems to have subsided. Leena moves to embrace him, but he pushes her back. She gives him a concerned but confused look.

The door opens and Max enters the room. Michael sits up and looks at Leena and then at Max.

MAX
Good to see you up and awake.

The silence is deafening.

MAX (cont.)
(concerned)
Chief, I...

MICHAEL
Max, don't. I know the truth now. I remember everything.
(a beat)
I'd like to talk to Leena alone now. Please leave us.

MAX
But...

MICHAEL
(firm but calm)

Please.

Max, somewhat disconsolate, turns and leaves, closing the door behind him. Leena looks at Michael, still confused. Michael looks at her and realizes he must try and explain what has happened.

MICHAEL (cont.)
That was Max Horton, my associate. Leena...

LEENA
Your associate? I don't understand. Michael, where have you been? The police... _I_ thought you'd been kidnapped...
murdered!
(pause)
Why do you look so different? What's going on here?

Michael sighs and leans forward in bed.

MICHAEL
Actually, he was Paul Sanderson's associate. This is his house.

LEENA
I... I don't understand.

MICHAEL
This is Paul Sanderson's home, and well, I'm Paul Sanderson.

Shock sets in. Leena doesn't understand a word Michael's saying, but listens on as he continues.

MICHAEL (cont.)
...and The Wraith.

LEENA
I don't understand. You're Michael Reeve not...

MICHAEL
As hard as this may be to understand...

I'm both of these men, Leena. You see, something happened to me the night I disappeared. Something amazing, something I understand and cannot comprehend at the same time. I'm both the recipient and instigator of this whole process.

Michael stands, and Leena now fully notices his chiseled physique. She looks stunned by this, but remains silent and seated. Michael takes a deep breath before continuing.

MICHAEL (cont.)
Sanderson was also The Wraith. He's real, the urban legend is real, and always has been. Somehow, someway, I...
(pause)
Sanderson passed everything on to me. His powers, memories, emotions... everything.

He looks at Leena as he grasps her hand in his.

MICHAEL (cont.)
I have become Paul Sanderson.

Leena throws his hand back.

LEENA
No!
(pause)
I can't believe what I'm hearing. You're Michael Reeve, not...

MICHAEL
I'm as much Paul Sanderson as I am Michael Reeve now.

LEENA
I don't know what to think about all of this. I don't know what to believe, Michael.

MICHAEL
I know, and I'm sorry to lay all of this on you, especially now. But you

need to know everything, you need to know the truth, and... telling you all this has somehow helped me come to terms with everything myself.

LEENA

What are you trying to tell me?

MICHAEL

I <u>am</u> Paul Sanderson... now and forever.

CUT TO:

INT. HALLWAY - NIGHT

Max Horton paces the floor in front of the bedroom door where Leena and Michael discuss their new life together.

Max steps beside the door as he hears Michael speak.

MICHAEL (VO)

I am Paul Sanderson... now and forever.

Max smiles subtly in approval, as he steps away from the door.

CUT TO:

INT. BEDROOM - NIGHT

Michael stands before Leena, his posture incredible and more defined than before. He's clearly a changed man, in more ways than one. He continues to try and explain the situation to a still very confused and clearly hurt Leena.

MICHAEL

I was part of my... Sanderson's backup plan. If anything were to happen to me... to him...

He pauses to gather his thoughts and let some of the incredible news seep in.

MICHAEL (cont.)

He chose me as his successor. This is so weird, Leena, I'm having trouble making sense of things myself, everything's just come back to me these last few minutes.

(pause)

I found his mask, or should I say he left it for me to find. Because of my belief in The Wraith and my ridicule for it, my lack of family, my constant wish to just help people as a police officer, he picked me. The research I... he did was incredible. And now I'm...

LEENA

You're Michael Reeve, the man I love more than life itself.

MICHAEL

But I'm so much more now. I'm two men at once, I have the lifetime memories of two people inside me.

This is all clearly too much for Leena to bear, she buries her face in her hands, and begins to cry.

LEENA

I didn't know what I had until I lost it... lost you. I love you so much and want you back... I need you.

MICHAEL

I love you too, but it's just not that simple anymore. I've changed and can't go back to what I was or what <u>we</u> were. And I can't ask you to come with me where I must go on this journey.

LEENA

I can't believe what I'm hearing. What are you saying to me?

Michael knows the pain he's causing her, but he also knows what has to be and what must be said.

MICHAEL
That Michael Reeve is dead. To you and the rest of the world. I must be... must remain Paul Sanderson.
(pause)
I'm sorry.

Leena cries, appears shell-shocked.

CUT TO:

INT. HALLWAY - NIGHT

Leena bursts from the bedroom and almost runs into Max. She scrambles off down the hall and through a door at the end.
Michael walks into the hallway casually and looks at Max.

MAX
Didn't take it well I see.

Michael looks at Max with a mixture of anger, hurt and determination.

MICHAEL
Max, don't... I understand why you and Sanderson did what you did. I know it was essential... but a part of me has a hard time forgiving you.

MAX
Chief...

MICHAEL
Keep an eye on her, I need to get out of here.

MAX
Is that a good idea?

Michael shoots Max a look, and Max knows not to press any further. Michael passes him as he walks down the corridor.

CUT TO:

INT. SANDERSON LIBRARY - NIGHT

EPIC LARRY GROUPÉ MUSIC BEGINS

CGI SEQUENCE

Michael strides into the darkened library, and stops before what appears in the darkness to be a large floor-to-ceiling bookcase. Michael pulls from his pocket a small remote control device and points it at the bookcase. With an audible HUM, the bookcase moves forward slightly, and slides to one side, revealing a dark, open doorway. Michael walks toward the open door and enters.

INT. THE WRAITH'S LAIR - NIGHT

Michael walks from the shadows into the light - he's now outfitted in the awesome The Wraith costume, save for the mask, which he holds in his hand. The amazing sight of the Lair dazzles us in the background.

Suddenly, the secret door slides open and Leena enters followed by Max.

END CGI SEQUENCE

MAX

She found her way down here, Chief. She was about to trash the place if I didn't take her to you. I thought it best...

MICHAEL

It's okay, Max.

Leena stands before Michael, looks at him in awe. He attaches the mask, and stands there, now having become The Wraith fully and completely. She gazes into his eyes.

LEENA

I'll be waiting for you when you return. We have a lot to talk about, Mr. Sanderson. I'm not going anywhere. If this is your life now, then I want... <u>need</u> to be a part of this.

She looks at him, and he knows when she's this determined, nothing on Earth can change her mind. Still, he tries.

THE WRAITH
You can't. My life is filled with danger. I can't give you what you need, I can't give you the security and future you deserve.

LEENA
What I need is <u>you</u>. Michael Reeve or Paul Sanderson... I need you!

The Wraith clenches his jaw, but realizes he cannot win, and really doesn't want to. He pauses... and makes a decision.

THE WRAITH
Leena, if you're serious, then there have to be changes. <u>I've</u> changed. For you to become a part of my life, <u>you</u> have to change as well.

Leena doesn't flinch at this.

LEENA
Anything.

THE WRAITH
To join me in my quest, you have to be able to assist me, whenever I may need you. You'll need to be able to do things you've never dreamed yourself capable of. Mentally, emotionally, and physically... you'll have to be able to hold your own and have my back just as Max does.
(pause)
Max will oversee your initial training, before you're ready to start training with me.

LEENA
Training?

THE WRAITH
Weights, gymnastics, martial arts, weaponry, criminology, mechanics, chemistry. You'll need a passing knowledge in all to be by my side.
(pause)
Are you sure you're ready for this?

Leena moves over to The Wraith and gently kisses him.

LEENA
I love you. I'll do anything to be a part of your life.

The Wraith briefly smiles before fully merging into his heroic, dour persona.

THE WRAITH
Stay with Max. I patrol alone tonight.

The Wraith turns and merges into the darkness at the back of the Lair. Max and Leena look on.

THE WRAITH (cont.)
(whispers to himself)
I love you too.

CUT TO:

EXT. ROOFTOP - NIGHT

The Wraith perched on the edge, listens for any sign of activity. He scans the city skyline like a perched eagle. (Possible greenscreen work here too?)

Arching his body, he throws his cape outward and leaps from the building edge.

CGI SEQUENCE

WIDE SHOT

The Wraith, using his cape as a parachute, glides to the street below. He lands with the grace and power of a bird of prey.

END CGI SEQUENCE

EXT. ALLEY - NIGHT

The Wraith rises from a crouch, looking eerie in the shadows, his cape wrapped around him. He scans his surrounds.

The radio in his cowl BEEPS quietly. He presses a spot on his temple and pauses to listen.

THE WRAITH
Yes?

MAX (VO)
Chief, I've got you on the GPS link-up. I've got Latham on the scope, out at Loeb Park, near the rundown industrial park. Advise investigation.

THE WRAITH
Understood.

The Wraith leaps over the fence at the end of the alley and vanishes into the night.

CUT TO:

EXT. BRIDGE - NIGHT

Robert Latham stands at the end of a small bridge located in Loeb Park, a small park, unkempt and overgrown with weeds. The old warehouse district of Metro City, rundown and a hive of criminal activity, can be seen in the background. A small, polluted creek flows slowly beneath the bridge.

Latham, lighting a cigar, waits impatiently. Alone.

From the opposite end, the Cobra steps from the shadows. Latham turns to face him.

LATHAM
Okay, I've flattered you by being here. What do you want? Why meet all the way out here?

THE COBRA
First, I want your assistant to step out and drop his piece.

Latham looks over his shoulder and motions to Grieco to step forward. Grieco, angry and hostile, appears and agrees to drop his weapon.

THE COBRA (cont.)
I have made a commitment to you, on good faith. But, it will come at a cost, a cost I will set at a time of my own choosing.

Grieco steps forward, can't believe what he's hearing.

GRIECO
Who is this loser? Are we going to let ourselves be dictated by him?!

LATHAM
(to the Cobra)
Why should I believe you capable of challenging The Wraith, let alone being able to kill him?

The Cobra steps a little closer in the light and we can see his marled eye and the Cobra-shaped scar. His face is menacing in the mixture of shadows and light.

THE COBRA
I'm not The Wraith's equal... I'm his superior! I have the strength and powers the like you could never imagine.

Grieco laughs derisively at the Cobra. He doesn't believe a word he's saying.

GRIECO
Mr Latham, are we seriously listening to this psycho?

Latham looks at the Cobra closely, and notices something.

LATHAM
(to Grieco)
Just wait.

The Cobra stares at Grieco, and a strange force begins to emanate from his marled eye.

THE COBRA
(to Grieco)
Pick up your gun!

Grieco does so, as if in some kind of a trance.

THE COBRA (cont.)
Now, place the gun to your temple... give your life in service to me.

Grieco does so and is about to pull the trigger...

LATHAM
NO!

THE COBRA
(points at Grieco)
STOP!

Grieco stops just in time, and stands silently to attention. The Cobra flashes an evil grin.

LATHAM
How did you do that? What the hell are you?

THE COBRA
In a way, I am <u>your</u> creation, Robert.
(pause)
The scepter and the parchment were the key. Great power to those who wield it and recite the ancient text.

Latham now realizes who this is, and reacts.

LATHAM
You...

THE COBRA
(ignoring Latham)
The expedition would have yielded the wisdom of the scepter, and even greater power. You had it all in your grasp, but your narrow-minded obsession with money, with profit, was your downfall.
(a beat)
Now, that ultimate power is mine!

LATHAM
(shocked)
My God!
(long pause)
Okay, you've proven yourself. Now, how are you going to take out that caped bastard?!

THE COBRA
It will be in a way you couldn't possibly comprehend. But it will be done. Do we have an accord?

The Cobra continues to smile devilishly at Latham, in a way that, combined with the surrounds, almost chills Latham to the bone.

LATHAM
I'll go along with you... for now. We have a deal. But I warn you...

Latham moves over to try and snap Grieco out of his daze, momentarily taking his eyes off the Cobra.

LATHAM (cont.)
...don't... fail me...

His words trail off as he turns to find the Cobra has gone. Latham and Grieco are alone.

The Cobra's voice rings out seemingly from nowhere, hypnotically.

THE COBRA (VO)
Just remember Robert... call me...

Latham and Grieco, now back to his senses, look at one another.

THE COBRA (VO, cont.)
...the Cobra.

And silence. Grieco rubs his temples, bewildered and with a headache.

GRIECO
What the hell just happened?

LATHAM
A deal with the devil... but quite possibly worth it.
(pause)
Now, let's not keep the Afghans waiting any longer. Time for the shipment to change hands.

Grieco starts to lead Latham away from the bridge, intending to head to their car.

CUT TO:

EXT. BRIDGE-TOP - NIGHT

The Wraith now sits perched atop the bridge, watching... and drops to the bridge floor.

EXT. BRIDGE - NIGHT

Both Latham and Grieco, not having gotten very far, turn at the sound behind them. The Wraith stands, ready for action and looking really pissed.

THE WRAITH
Latham! Your shipment of arms will not reach its destination! The police have already dealt with the terrorists you were consorting with.

Latham looks shocked and furious.

LATHAM
So, you <u>are</u> alive. I don't know how you survived that bullet, or how you derailed my arms deal, but it doesn't matter. I've just ensured your days on this Earth are numbered.

THE WRAITH
I doubt that.

LATHAM
Still, I did anticipate your visiting me tonight, and made full provisions. If bullets don't seem to faze you, try some of my fighters on for size.

Latham signals, and three of his bodyguards appear from the bushes, looking tough and meaning business.

CLOSE ON

We see The Wraith size up his three opponents. He lowers his gaze, readies himself and awaits their attack.

PAN BACK

The bodyguards quickly reach him. The Wraith leaps into the air at the last second and grabs a support beam over his head. Extending his legs, he wraps them around one of the thug's necks and spins. The bodyguard spins like a top in the air just before hitting the ground hard.

The Wraith lands to deal with the other two head on. He dodges a weak blow, sidesteps, and delivers an uppercut that would make Lennox Lewis piss himself. The second thug falls silent.

The third starts to kick, and actually kicks The Wraith... once. The Wraith grabs his leg directly after being kicked and swings the guy like a bat toward the edge of the bridge. The thug lands with a sickening impact, bouncing off of the side support beam and to the floor. The Wraith steps back and sizes up the situation.

Grieco, furious, pulls his piece and fires. The Wraith flips forward, dodging the bullets. Enraged and not thinking straight, Grieco throws his pistol to the ground and launches himself at The Wraith.

The Wraith spins, sweeping Grieco's legs and sending him crashing to his back.

From the ground, Grieco reaches for a second pistol on his person. He manages to just pull it out, but The Wraith kicks it from his grasp. He punches Grieco hard on the nose, sending him to sleepy land.

The Wraith now stands erect, and faces a retreating Latham head-on.

LATHAM (cont.)
You son of a bitch!

The Wraith grabs Latham by his hair and forces him to look into the 'eyes of judgment,' which glow ominously on The Wraith's chest.

Latham pulls free holding his face. He screams in agony, only to turn the scream into a psychotic laugh. The Wraith looks a little surprised.

LATHAM (cont.)
Your mind games won't work on me. I'm not the usual dimestore hood you take out.

By way of reply, The Wraith smashes a powerful right into Latham's stomach, followed by a knee to the crimelord's face, breaking his nose. Latham bounces off the bridge railing and staggers to remain standing. He holds his bleeding face, looks up at The Wraith with hatred and contempt.

LATHAM (cont.)
You'll die slowly for that!

The Wraith pulls back to punch again, but notices...

...Grieco, back on his feet and stupid enough to want to continue. He cracks his knuckles and gets into his fighting stance. He steps forward driving punches and kicks furiously at The Wraith. The Wraith blocks all of the blows, they're weak and Grieco is ill-skilled. He lets the deputy go, wearing himself out.

Tired, The Wraith sees his opportunity and takes it. Grieco throws a weak right and The Wraith grabs his fist dead on. He applies pressure almost crushing Grieco's hand. Grieco drops to his knees, whimpering in pain.

The Wraith draws back and releases a devastating left to Grieco's chin, ending the battle once-and-for-all.

THE WRAITH
You're finished.

GRIECO
(barely conscious)
Go to Hell!

The Wraith punches him again, sending Grieco to the ground, bleeding and unconscious.

Latham pulls himself up weakly and stares at The Wraith. Bleeding, hatred still nevertheless registers strongly on his face, burning with a newfound brilliance.

LATHAM
You may be able to defeat my men, you may be able to take me down one day... but I tell you, from this night on, your time in this city is finished! You're a dead man!

The Wraith smirks briefly, but says nothing.

The first bodyguard wakes and rises behind The Wraith. He holds a knife aloft, as if ready to stab The Wraith in the back. Without looking, The Wraith throws a reverse forearm punch behind him, knocking the thug out. The Wraith now faces Latham down.

THE WRAITH

Let this night be a warning to you. Your days running this city as though it were your own personal empire are coming to an end. I will be watching you. Every day could be your last. Judgment is coming!

(pause)

Now, take your filth and crawl back to your hole.

Grieco stirs and moves as quickly as possible, at Latham's barking orders, to rouse the three bodyguards.

The Wraith swirls his cloak over and in front of the camera... darkness... (possible cgi here?)

CUT TO:

EXT. ROOFTOP - NIGHT

The Wraith is perched again looking down on the city. He scans the skyline of his city.

THE WRAITH

(narration)

Metro City... a hive of evil and corruption. But good people still live here... I do what I do for them, for the helpless, the besieged. The battle tonight was won, but the war... the war goes on.

CLOSE ON

The Wraith's face, his eyes, heroic and determined...

DISSOLVE TO:

INT. SECRET LOCATION - NIGHT

The dissolve transforms The Wraith's eyes into the Cobra's eyes, distinguished by the right, milky white eye.

PULL BACK

The Cobra, sitting regally on a chair looking almost like a throne, smiles devilishly, stares into the darkness before him. A single light above him shines eerily down.

He leans forward.

THE COBRA
(to himself)
Metro City will soon be mine, as destiny has pre-ordained. The Wraith will fall, as will all those who oppose me. A war is coming. And I will be the one left standing, to grind The Wraith and Robert Latham's bones into the dust!

He laughs, slowly at first, building into a crescendo, as we...

CUT TO: BLACK

His laugh can still be heard as it...

FADES INTO:

END WITH MANDI LEIGH'S 'HOME OF DARKNESS' LOVE SONG AND CREDITS

THE WRAITH
Eyes of Judgment

The Interviews

Conducted by

A.P. Fuchs

Stephen Semones,
Director of *The Wraith: Eyes of Judgment*

Stephen Semones, Head of Sir Reel Films, Speaks Out

APF: When did you start working on *The Wraith: Eyes of Judgment*?

SS: I met Frank Dirscherl in early August of 2003 on a message forum. He posted a proposal for an Independent Filmmaker to have the option of making a movie based on his Independent Comic Book Character. After a brief "get to know you" session, Frank and I hit it off and he asked me to take the project on. I began working on the script and learned everything I could about this unknown character. Having read comics my whole life, I felt that this was my shot at something great, something wonderful. We began principal filming in February of 2004 and wrapped in June of 2005. When the film premieres, it will have been over two years in the making and will be debuting on my 28th birthday this August 19th.

APF: I'm a fan of independent comics myself so I can understand the appeal. But for yourself, what was it about The Wraith character that made you decide, "Yes, I want to do this," and put all this time and effort into the project?

SS: When I saw the character I was taken aback by his commanding presence. It was like seeing a more realistic superhero. That's what we've tried to portray with the film. Once I read Frank's novel and comic, I knew that I had to do this film. The main reason I wanted to do it was because it was a comic book film and each character is so involved and deep that it's good as a filmmaker to have such substance to work with. Also we knew going into this that we wouldn't have a big studio choosing actors or special FX over the story. The story is the main reason I chose to do this film though. It's a very complex and powerful story. Each character has a reason to exist in Frank's world and they all are very grounded. There's a new superhero on the block and we hope to touch people with his story.

APF: So what was the first step once you and Frank agreed to do a film?

SS: The first step was for me to research and understand each aspect of the world Frank created. Once I was able to understand what The Wraith was all about, I began working on a script. I based the script from the first two issues of the comic and first half of the novel. One vital step was the decision to include The Cobra villain. Frank has never told his origin so to have him in the film, we had to create one specifically. Frank gave me the go-ahead to develop that portion of the film. When writing the script, I had to basically become each character in order to fully bring them to life. I wrote the script in basically a month then Frank and I sent it back and forth [further] fleshing it out. Two months after we decided to make the film, we had a great shooting script. The next step was casting for a comic book film with absolutely no budget.

APF: Thus is the way of independent filmmaking. How'd you convince the actors to work for free?

SS: Convincing the actors took very little effort after they read the script. They all loved it and wanted to be a part of the film regardless of what they'd be doing. I did however work out contracts with each one to ensure they'd all get a percentage of DVD sales.

APF: Was it a challenge arranging everybody's shooting schedule? I know movies are shot out of order then pieced together later.

SS: It was incredibly tough. It literally took us almost two whole years to make a 45-minute film due to the cast and crew having regular jobs, and everyone's schedule. Sometimes we'd have a call for four actors and all but one could shoot the day of filming. Then when that actor was available, someone else wasn't, so it became a tough and challenging task arranging the shooting schedules.

APF: But you and your team prevailed. That says a lot as most independent film projects go under, scheduling conflicts being one of the main reasons. How did you guys work the FX shots? I know a lot of the movie was shot on green screen. Any challenge in working on a set that "wasn't there"?

SS: The challenges to working with a green screen and special FX is the same old story you hear from everyone: "There's little to work with or reference. Too much imagination has to be used." Well, the main problem we had (as we had the whole film) was budget. Our problems were the same as everyone else—imagination—but had we had a bigger budget the shoot would have been smoother. We had it rough from the beginning only having one camera to film with.

Once we got into the groove of working with an eleven foot by twenty foot screen hanging from a warehouse ceiling, the imagination wasn't too hard to come by. Using the comic and other photos from Frank as reference material, the actors were able to envision what the final product would look like.

Learning where to place the camera and having to imagine where the CG would be was an obstacle, but we soon got over it. After a while, it becomes routine and no one thinks about not having a location to shoot on. The hardest task for me personally has to be getting the actors to understand the dimensions for the shot; where they'll be placed and how much room they have to move and why. It becomes a difficult task getting everything just right. If I were just starting out making films I would stay away from using a green screen. It literally adds a whole new layer to your work and can be very costly.

APF: Was the FX shots being compiled while you were shooting or did you shoot everything first then add the FX?

SS: We would shoot the FX stuff and edit it into scene form. Then I would send the scene to our FX wizard, Marc Kimball, and he would add the FX and send the scene back. I ended up sending Marc a total of three or four shipments of footage for him to work on over the course of several months. I would have completed FX edited into the film as he was working on more scenes. For the cut I was using, I would temporarily use the non-FX cut of the scene for timing and scene placement and replace it once I got the completed footage.

APF: Was August 2nd, 2005 always the envisioned release date or was it more of an "Okay, we'll work on a film and when it's done it's done and we'll set a release from there"?

SS: Well, the release date has changed several times since August of 2003, but once Frank realized he was releasing the novel on August 2nd, we decided to shoot for that date. The film will be done by then, but we had to push the release forward until August 19th due to scheduling at the Cinemall. If we open the week of August 2nd, we'll be going up against two decent-sized Hollywood movies at the time and the Cinemall's owner, Steve Weston, suggested we push it back two weeks. The whole production we knew we had an estimate of three to four months once we wrapped shooting until we premiered, so we've kind of had that in the back of our minds from the beginning.

APF: Sounds like a good plan. Keeping the focus on *The Wraith* will have more of an impact than sharing it with other films. Is this your first release at the Cinemall or have any other Sir Reel Film flicks been released there in the past?

SS: No, this is the very first time any of our films have premiered on the big screen. It's very exciting to know that our film gets a world premiere at such a prestigious theater. I'm honored to have my film debut at the Cinemall.

APF: Progress is the name of the game. Back to the creation of the film, did you draw on any examples/techniques from other movies when shooting *The Wraith*?

SS: I watched a lot of comic book films throughout the filming. Good and bad, I watched basically every comic book film ever made in order to see what not to do and see if there was a way for us to tell this [the story] in an original fashion. I drew a lot of inspiration for the camera angles and shots from Peter Jackson, Robert Rodriguez, and Sam Raimi. Those three filmmakers use amazing camera shots and watching their films is like attending film school. I watched a lot of movies for camera shot ideas but a lot of them came on the fly as we were filming. I would set up the scene with the actors and then find the best place to film it from. Sometimes the storyboards were rendered useless and we just went with what felt best for the scene. This is where I'd bring in camera styles or techniques from other directors. We'd usually have a shot or angle set up and then we'd sit and talk about how to make it work better. Needless to say, a lot of camera work seen in *The Wraith* will take your breath.

APF: Can't wait! When composing a trailer for a film—and as recently spoofed in the trailer for Hitchhiker's Guide to the Galaxy—was there a certain formula you followed? Example: First select a scene that'll grab their interest then...

SS: Not really. I mean, to me a trailer has to just grab you from all angles. Sometimes you already know how you're going to piece the trailer together and sometimes it's a process of elimination. To decide the opening shot to grab the audience for a trailer is tough. It usually changes several times before you release it. Once you replay the trailer and get a feel for it overall, then you go back and make the necessary changes. Usually you like one piece in the middle and work from there.

To me, the hardest part is not showing too much too soon or not enough at all. A trailer has to be balanced and tease the audience into wanting to watch your film. If you don't give enough away or give too much away, the audience will react negatively to it. You have to find a good balance, which is tough, and stick with it through the whole trailer.

APF: I understand you just came back from a comic book convention and had a Sir Reel Films/Trinity Comics table there. What was people's reaction to The Wraith there?

SS: The reaction was very positive. Everyone seemed to love the trailer from the film and the comic. We sold out of comics by half way through the second day, so it went very well. John Rhys-Davies, Adam West, and Jackson Bostwick (Captain Marvel) all thought the comic was really cool and what we were doing was inventive and special. Having these respected actors praise us was truly mind-blowing and spectacular.

APF: I'll bet. What about the fans, those in attendance at the convention. What did they think?

SS: Refreshing. A lot of people in attendance live near me, so they see me as a local bringing something [in]to the region. The fact of The Wraith being an independent comic book didn't seem to bother them, as most people would pass it over in a comic shop in favor for a more well-known book. We helped bridge the gap of being unfamiliar with The Wraith.

The reaction to the character was steady throughout the weekend: everyone was happy to see something new and fresh to the scene. The reaction was positive and I think Frank picked up several new readers.

APF: Good news. More people should know about this character. What do you hope to gain from the film's release, personally and professionally?

SS: I agree. More people should know about The Wraith. I had to become each character in order to write the script, so I've already got to know myself better through writing and filming. I grew as a filmmaker on this film and learned so much. That much I've already gained.

What I hope to gain with the release personally is the sense of satisfaction. We set out to make a comic book movie and saw it through to the end. We had a hell of a ride the whole time and releasing it is truly bittersweet. It's so personal to me and you can actually see me grow as a director on this film.

Professionally I hope to gain enough trust by the right people and have them finance our films. I've got loads of stories waiting to be told and I hope someone has enough faith in me to allow me the chance to tell them. With this film I hope Sir Reel Films is recognized for its achievement as a whole and we are all elevated to the next level of filmmaking. So many people gave so much for this film that I can't just talk about my career alone. I guess the heat falls on me mostly, but everyone gave 200% and I hope they're all recognized for their efforts and hard work as well.

APF: Well, I wish you the best come release day and beyond. Growing up, were you a comic book fan or is that something more recent?

SS: I grew up reading comics: *Batman*, *Spider-man*, *X Men*, *The Punisher*. Those were my favorites to read as a kid. I think my first comic was a Batman comic, to be exact. I've continually read comics throughout my life and still enjoy them. I don't have as much time to put into reading them now, but I still love them. I even have a Spider-man tattoo.

APF: From the character names you've mentioned, it's easy to say The Wraith, though he doesn't have the same extensive history, is on par with those characters. I'm a huge fan of new superheroes, those created in the small press community and those that aren't published by DC or Marvel. It is my belief that the future of superheroes, though it may take awhile, will be spawned by the small press. There's something very earnest and authentic about them that I find charming. How do you feel about the independent comic market and, more importantly, the independent film market, whether those films be superhero or otherwise? How do they compare to the big boys?

SS: I agree with you. The future of new superheroes lies in the hands of the small press. I hope to play a small part and give hope to others trying to get their [respective] superhero recognition.

To be honest, I feel that we're breaking ground with *The Wraith*. It takes a small group of dreamers to change the world, and though that's not our goal, we'd like to play a part in changing how movies are made. The independent market for film and comics are very similar. It's like an exclusive club and you watch from the outside hoping to get in for that secret handshake. It's not that extreme, but that's basically it. It's hard for struggling comic publishers and filmmakers to make it with the "big boys" and a lot give up after a brief time. They feel their time will never come, so the indie markets on both fronts are constantly changing. People come and go and the ones that press on regardless of "making it" are the ones who succeed in the long run.

As far as making a superhero film, Hollywood usually handles those. Sir Reel Films and Trinity Comics hope to prove to people that Hollywood no longer has control over the superhero market. Everything is going digital and it's a lot easier for indie filmmakers to now jump in and start making movies. However, very few of them succeed because they do not promote their films properly. Indie comic publishers suffer the same type of fate. Because of technology rapidly advancing, both film and comics are in the hands of independent artists. A lot of people just simply give up halfway through or after one comic or film. They see it as an exclusive club and walk away with shattered dreams.

Making *The Wraith*, the whole time we all stated many times that this film is for the up and coming filmmakers with dreams of making it big and have no idea where to start. To paraphrase Robert Rodriguez "...if you have a camera, you're already halfway there to being a filmmaker. The next thing you need is something to film. Film what you know and keep it tight." The same can apply to indie comic publishers. Very few stick with a character like The Wraith and it's sad that most new comic characters that are worthy will never have their shot on film.

APF: I understand what you mean. Many small presses do come and go and it's namely to do with financial hardships. But, like you said, it's the ones that forge ahead that are the ones that succeed. What do you plan to do with *The Wraith* film once it's released to prove to Hollywood that you've made a quality superhero flick and that it's going places?

SS: Premiering it at the Abingdon Cinemall will help. After that it's basically film festivals and conventions to gain publicity. The hardest thing about making an indie film is getting the film out there to people. Once we have the premiere, we'll be touring the festival and convention circuit with the film. In September, we're releasing the DVD so word of mouth should soon spread about our film.

APF: Word of mouth is also the best means of marketing, if the product is great which, of course, I know *The Wraith* is. When making the film, what was one of the biggest challenges? And what was one of the greatest successes?

SS: One of the greatest challenges was trying to make a comic book movie. That was a challenge in itself. Just thinking above and beyond the usual method of [superhero] thinking was hard to get over. We all had to think outside the box on this film.

As far as our greatest success, I'd have to say it was seeing the film through to the end. We've had our ups and downs but overall, it's been a complete joyride and seeing it through to the end is a great achievement.

APF: Well done. Were there any mishaps or humorous moments while making the film that come readily to mind?

SS: There was a lot of fun happening on set most of the time. Usually someone [was] always joking around to pass the time. Several scenes were interrupted and we have quite the blooper reel. As far as mishaps go, there were a couple. Joey Hale, who plays Otto the thug in the opening scene, he hurt his big toe rehearsing for a scene we were about to shoot. During some of the film you can notice a slight limp from him. He gave it all he had though and you can barely even notice it, but he is in pain.

During the final fight scene, my brother David, who plays Charlie Grieco, had his gun stripped from him during the scene and he was literally pistol whipped. We ended up using the take, so when he gets smacked, he really got smacked. His head got cut open, but it wasn't bad. He was back in front of the camera within ten minutes ready to go. When you see him get slapped and he goes down, it's for real. His bell had been rung.

As far as any other mishaps, there were the cuts, bruises, scrapes that come along with anything you film that's like this. Everyone was really dedicated to the film and didn't let anything like pain come between them and the movie.

APF: Well, pain is beauty, right? Do you make a cameo in the film?

SS: Yes, I actually have two cameos in the film. The first one I actually have a conversation with the character Michael Reeve and deliver something very important to him. Oh yeah, did I mention the character I played was Dutch the Bum?

To get into character for the bum, I didn't shave for a week and rolled around in the dirt before we shot. I got into character and really had fun with it. David Cooper (The Wraith) even talked me into doing that role. He enjoys playing off me onscreen and wanted me to do something with him.

As far as my other cameo, I played a henchman to Robert Latham. No big deal there except that I'm in a crucial scene with The Wraith. I don't want to spoil too much there, but it's not hard to figure out which henchman I am.

APF: I always love it when the director makes an appearance. Good form. How did David Cooper like moving around in the suit?

SS: He didn't like it at all. He and I go back to ninth grade (like, 15 years ago) and you can say I've known him over half my life; however, no matter how long we have known one another, he still wasn't happy about wearing the suit. He got through it and it wasn't as bad as he'll tell you it was, but it wasn't pleasant either.

The suit was molded from a wetsuit and had polyurethane armor molded to it. It added about fifteen to eighteen pounds of excess baggage to him. On top of that, it was extremely hot inside it. He was limited around his knees and feet as far as being able to move them easily. His shoulders didn't give much in the suit either. The weight of the suit was basically on his shoulders.

One night after filming, we took the suit off of him and he began to steam when his body hit the cold air. You could literally see the steam all over him. It usually took about two or three people just to help him in the suit. It usually took only one to help him remove it because he was so eager [to take it off]; he'd be pulling it off as he walked off set. He would constantly sweat in the suit and he'd be constantly thirsty. It was really tough on him physically, especially during the fight scenes. Usually on those, after about two takes he was breaking to towel off and get water.

The Wraith costume was one complete piece, including the cape, which we'd flip over the front to get him in. Getting his legs in was the hardest and most challenging aspect. Once we got his legs in, we'd lift it up his front and slide his arms in while pulling it over his shoulders. Then we'd flip the cape over his head, resting it down his back. Then came the boots and belt. After that we'd slide the gauntlets up his arms. The cowl was always put on last. We'd black his eyes and then put on the cowl. Putting on the suit was almost a ritual each time we did it. The cowl going on would symbolize he was ready to film in the suit. It was made of rubber, so needless to say that he would sweat profusely and the black paint around his eyes would almost blind him. It zipped up in the back, under the cape, and once we unzipped him we'd have to peel the suit off of him.

The funny thing about the suit is that Xtreme Design FX created the whole suit from David's measurements that I emailed them. The first time they met him, they handed us the suit.

APF: Kind of like how Clooney and Kilmer expressed wearing the Bat-suit. Good thing, if superheroes were real, they wouldn't wear rubber-armor. So be honest—did you ever steal the mask and try and it on just to see what you'd look like or how you'd feel?

SS: Yeah, I put it on when Xtreme first delivered it. After that it got really sweaty and gross, so I didn't even consider it again. However, I did get a laugh when people would see it for the first time and immediately put the cowl on. They'd ask me why I was laughing and my response would be for them to smell it.

APF: Looking back on the movie, was there anything you might have done differently or any big lesson learned that you can carry into the next project?

SS: There are a lot of things I'd like to have done differently, but that can apply with anything really. The biggest lesson I learned was how to make a comic book movie. Cheaply, that is. I mean, for the budget and then what we achieved, it's a miracle. I'm hoping to take all the filmmaking knowledge I got on this film into my next film and so on. I learned so much, it's really hard to single out one thing.

APF: What is the next project?

SS: It's a horror film called *faiTh*. It's a cross between *The Exorcist* and *The Amittyville Horror*. That's basically all I'm at liberty to say right now. Usual Sir Reel people will be involved, but this will be our first feature film.

APF: Horror. Right up my alley. What else do you do when you're not making films?

SS: Well, I have a beautiful wife of almost six years and a son that's about to turn five, so I try to spend as much time as possible with them. Other than that, to relax I play Xbox or just simply watch movies. I love to read and listen to music as well. Sometimes I'll just write when I have free time, so I guess what I do really depends on the mood I'm in, but I strive to put my family first.

APF: If you were to sum up *The Wraith: Eyes of Judgment* in one word, what would it be?

SS: Ambitious.

Frank Dirscherl, the man behind The Wraith.

Frank Dirscherl, Publisher of Trinity Comics, Talks About His Creation, The Wraith

APF: The Wraith was thought up when, precisely?

FD: I created The Wraith one afternoon back in 1998 after having read a *Spider* pulp novel. I was trying to come up with my own version of the Spider and a rough picture of The Wraith was then born.

APF: Did you draw him? If so, how did he first turn out?

FD: A friend of mine drew him up, but he looked like a combination of Spawn and (Legion of Superheroes character) Timberwolf at the time. As I was not looking to take the character any further at that stage, I left it at that.

APF: So when did it pick up again?

FD: The character bounced around in my head for a couple years. In 1999 or 2000, I tried my hand at writing a novel. I got a few pages in and it sounded exactly like a Spider pulp novel except with the names changed. I couldn't get my head around it until 2002 when then Alliance Comics publisher Shane Melton and I met online.

APF: Did Alliance Comics first publish *The Wraith* before you did with your own Trinity Comics? What was their reaction to the character?

FD: Shane Melton and I re-designed the character's look for publication as a 4-issue comic book mini-series in late 2002. Despite going through some artist setbacks, we were able to get one issue completed and ready for publication, when Alliance fell apart.

So, we had an issue ready and we were left out in the cold, which is when I formed Trinity Comics and began preparing to start from scratch and publish *The Wraith* on my own. Melton loved the character and the scripts I had written, and *The Wraith* was intended as Alliance's spearhead title before their collapse.

APF: So what happened to that completed issue that was to be published by Alliance?

FD: It was never published. I have the page files still, safely stored away. I wasn't happy with the quality of the art and halfway through, the original inker had to complete the pencils and the change shows badly. So, setting up Trinity Comics actually turned out to be the best thing for the character.

APF: That's too bad. Maybe one day it'll be republished. So was it around this time you thought about doing a film? I mean, aside from the daydreaming most creators do when thinking their comic would make a killer film.

FD: That story is being published, as *The Wraith* #1, due out later this year, with art by our brilliant penciler Jim Taylor. I always think/dream big. I'm always looking for opportunities to take The Wraith to bigger, better places. Books, merchandising, toys, animation, film. I started looking into the film option in 2003.

APF: How did you find the collaboration process with Stephen Semones on *The Wraith: Eyes of Judgment*? By this point, you weren't a stranger to teaming up with someone but you worked mainly in comics when doing that. Film is a different arena. From what he told me, he wrote the screenplay then showed you and then you two bounced it back and forth until it was good. How does Stephen's original script compare to the final script you two worked on?

FD: I met Stephen on a film message board online, and after talking with him, I knew he understood the character. He got it. I can't overstate that—so many directors, big and small, don't. So, I found our collaboration very smooth and easy going. Basically, Stephen wrote the first draft, I wrote the second, which was also the last. Two drafts were all we needed. I changed some character's dialogue, to match portions of the comic and novel, and switched a couple scenes around. Roughly speaking, the first quarter or so is mostly Stephen's, the rest is largely my re-worked material.

APF: Okay, so I misunderstood. Since you two live in different countries, how did you manage the collaboration once filming began?

FD: Well, again, because Stephen understood the character so well, our collaboration went very well indeed. Stephen and I would email each other constantly, we'd talk on AOL IM regularly, we'd update each other with what each other was doing. I can say there were many late nights on both sides, but I'm so pleased and proud with how well we worked together during the whole process.

APF: What was your reaction when he first showed you some footage from the film?

FD: It's been such a long journey so far—two years all up and counting.

If I remember correctly, the first scene I was shown was between Robert Latham and his deputy Charlie Grieco, and I was very impressed. Rick McVey is a theater professional, and the spitting image of how I pictured the character, so I was very impressed and delighted by that first scene.

APF: Did he send you a handful of completed scenes at a time or did he send you whatever footage they had after shooting and you had to kind of picture what the final scene would look like?

FD: It varied. Stephen would usually show me one scene at a time, but I still haven't seen the film in its entirety (i.e. every completed scene). I would usually be shown first a rough setup of a particular scene, without final editing, sound effects, visual effects or music score. Then, visual effects supervisor Marc Kimball would show me the scene with the visual effects added, and we're now waiting on the sound effects and music score to come through.

APF: Did you have to approve each scene before they would consider it as part of the final film or did you let them have creative control and what they showed you was what you got?

FD: I was happy with the scenes I saw and therefore didn't really need to approve anything. I would offer suggestions and ideas where I thought appropriate and where I thought they were needed, and these were always taken onboard.

APF: I know for myself I'm pretty sticky on my creations. Even when I have someone design a cover for one of my books, I'm pretty clear on what I'd like to see. Were there times where you had trouble letting go and trusting Stephen to deliver a good product? Honestly.

FD: Honestly? Not really. I knew going into this it would be very low budget, so I went into the project with open eyes. I did insist on a professional looking Wraith costume and I was able to help the project achieve a certain quality by bringing various crew members onboard, and I made some suggestions regarding the ending of the film, but other than that, I let Stephen work his magic.

APF: And Stephen pulled it off. When do you get your screening of *The Wraith: Eyes of Judgment*. You're in Australia and Stephen's in the States. Do you get to see if before August 2, 2005?

FD: I honestly don't know when I'll get to see it exactly. In August sometime, I think.

APF: What do you think your reaction will be? Do you have any expectations?

FD: I'll be excited and extremely proud with all the hard work the boys have put into it. For such a low budget, the film has turned out very well indeed, and it looks like it cost much more than it did. I'm proud of that.

APF: Great! Wish I could be there when you first lay eyes on it. Are there talks for a second film?

FD: I'm dying to see it, but patience is a virtue. We're hopeful of getting funding for a feature film based on what we've achieved with the short film. Fingers crossed.

APF: Do you know how Sir Reel Films finances its films?

FD: Through Stephen's own finances I believe, but he'll be better placed to answer that question.

APF: Fair enough. What are your current plans for The Wraith after the film and the dust jacket hardcover re-release of your novel?

FD: Work hard on getting the next issue of *The Wraith* comic book, *The Wraith* #1, to print, and then tackle the novel's sequel, *Valley of Evil.*

APF: Do you know when we can expect the next comic?

FD: In time for the Supanova Pop Culture Expo in October.

APF: Switching gears, how did your friends and family react when you went about creating The Wraith and turning it into a franchise?

FD: Everyone's been hugely supportive, especially my family and girlfriend. I couldn't have achieved what little I have without them. My friends are proud of my recent publishing deal; they keep telling me I'm going to be a star...something I keep trying to dissuade them from saying.

APF: But you never know, Frank. The secret to success always lies in how badly you want something and what you're willing to do to get there. The Wraith is a great character. I especially like the idea that he's kind of two guys in one, the way Paul Sanderson transferred himself onto Michael Reeve. Did anything inspire that idea? It's not exactly a normal thing for most heroes to have undergone.

FD: I'm not mercenary or cutthroat enough, but I will work hard to get The Wraith out there as best as I can to the best of my abilities. [The two guys in one] That was just an idea I had to make him as original as possible. In thinking up the character, he's clearly from the pulp magazine arena, and the two-characters-in-one idea had never been done to my knowledge in that genre.

APF: The only thing that might be considered similar is how Firestorm is that kid and the professor all in one. That's the only "two-in-one" I can think of, but that's still completely different from The Wraith. The villains, Robert Latham, reminds me of Lex Luthor, in that he's your powerful billionaire with the kind public front whose secretly bent on taking over the world. Was he a tip of the hat to the famous villain?

FD: In the comics world, there are similarities everywhere, if you look for them. With Latham, I wanted The Wraith's villain to be an everyday guy, albeit one with incredible power (and by power, I mean influence in a business and political sense), to offset all the fantastic villains that I intend to introduce later. I also wanted to touch upon a future power struggle between the old hat boss (Latham) and his young gun deputy, Charlie Grieco, which will slowly come to the fore. Luthor never came to my mind when creating Latham.

APF: Speaking of fantastical villains, the one currently introduced is The Cobra. What inspired him?

FD: No one character inspired the Cobra, though I guess his closest pulp counterpart would be Shadow villain Shiwan Khan. The Cobra has just one aim—to conquer. He enjoys the challenge, the slaughter, the pain. He revels in it. He's really my updated version of someone like Genghis Khan (as Shiwan Khan was in the Shadow pulps).

APF: Is there any chance you can give us a sneak peek into any upcoming super villains to grace the pages of *The Wraith*?

FD: The sequel novel, *Valley of Evil*, sees the introduction of rival crimelord Ma Tzi, as well as femme fatale Natalya Blackova (who has links with the Cobra as shown in the first novel), who unleashes a deadly virus on Metro City. The comics will see an evil cult worshipping a painting which can kill, a werewolf, a shape-shifting swamp witch, an imposter Wraith and more, while Robert Latham continues plotting behind the scenes.

APF: You're giving me goose bumps. Managing The Wraith is obviously a very busy task. How do you manage your time?

FD: I try and make the time. I don't work full time, so that helps, but even in the weeks when I do work most/all days, I make sure to put in some time in the evenings/nights. It can get tiring, but I believe in what I'm doing and having fun as well. That counts for a lot.

APF: And it's that perseverance that will make all the difference in the end. But let's get down to The Wraith character. We talked a bit about him being two people in one in an almost literal sense, but why does The Wraith do what he does? Every hero has a motivation, one bigger than "they're just a good person." Why a costume? How did he get his powers (or is that a secret for now)?

FD: Yes, the secret hows and whys of Paul Sanderson obtaining his powers must be kept a secret...for now. I plan to cover that one day, but I think it's a character strength to not reveal everything right at the outset. Suffice it to say, he received his powers while on his world travels (as outlined in *The Wraith* #0 comic book). Sanderson, while on his travels to find himself and find meaning in his life, saw the horrors of life for so many evil dictators in Africa and Asia, starvation, disease running rampant, and he knew the purpose he'd been searching for for so long, ever since childhood, was to help people.

So, he decided to start in his own backyard. Metro City. The costume made sense to shield his identity; [also] to be comfortable and functional and for protection.

APF: I guess it wouldn't be good if folks knew a billionaire was a superhero. Is there a reason Paul Sanderson is such a recluse? I mean, as you state in your novel, he's just as notorious as J.D. Salinger for not appearing in the public eye.

FD: The original Sanderson had no personal life. Once he became The Wraith, that was his entire life. He saw no purpose in doing anything else. He had no family, no loved ones, so he simple eschewed any semblance of a personal life and focused all his energies on his life's mission. This is more or less covered in *The Wraith* #0 comic book. The new Paul Sanderson, however, is a different matter.

APF: Since Michael Reeve is now the "new" Paul Sanderson, will there be any relapses to his old life? What I mean is, since he still has his memories as Michael Reeve, will there come a point where he has a good hard look at being, essentially, three people: Michael Reeve, Paul Sanderson and The Wraith?

FD: Michael has accepted both personas into his life with harmony. After the initial shock, the blending is smooth. He has memories of both lives, but it somehow works. So, there's nothing to look at; it is as it is.

APF: Do you have any particular routine when sitting down to write a Wraith story? Any habits? Any methods?

FD: No, I'm pretty boring. No routine, no habits or methods. I just sit down when I have the time and write. Can be any part of the day. It really depends on my work schedule with the library.

APF: Is there a particular direction you're taking the story?

FD: Just high adventure in the pulp tradition.

APF: Are there any themes you'd like to cover? I know when Todd McFarlane did his run on Spider-man, he had an issue where he looked at racism. With *The Wraith*, is there anything particular you want to say or a view you'd like to express?

FD: No, I don't want to get into politics or current affairs or anything like that. The Wraith is purely about adventure. It's a pulp magazine brought to life in 2005. High octane adventure, romance and melodrama. I don't want to politicize or date these stories, or stray from its pulp roots.

APF: In comics today, what are they getting right and what, in your opinion, are they doing wrong?

FD: Comics today are a pretty boring lot. Unfortunately, ego is running riot, and weak editorial teams are allowing creators to do whatever they please, whether it's right or responsible or not. Sales are down across the board and management believes gimmicks and extreme stories (killing off characters, changing their fundamental make-ups, etc.) will equal increased sales, but it never works long term. Comic book art is at its best, though, on many titles, but unfortunately storytelling isn't following suit. That's really a prime reason why I wanted to write my own stories and do them my own way, a way of bringing back the quality comic books of the 70s and 80s back to audiences.

APF: What do you think is the biggest challenge facing aspiring comic book creators today?

FD: It's always been a hard industry to break into, but even more so today. The big companies (i.e. DC, Marvel, Image) aren't particularly interested in nurturing new talent; they're happy to sign up as many big names as they can in a battle to outdo each other. The good thing is there are plenty of smalltime publishers where up-and-coming talent can get their chance to be creative, but it's a long hard slog, years of hard work to get into the big time, and even then there are no guarantees. The best thing I can say is, if it's something you want badly enough, then keep at it and never give up.

APF: I'm of the same mind. It's all about perseverance and passion. Those who want it enough do get it and they do whatever it takes to get there. Sure, splash-in-the-pan successes and overnight stars occur, but those are few and far between. They also happen to be the ones we hear about, too. As I had mentioned to Stephen when speaking with him about The Wraith, I am convinced the future of comics, books and film lies in the independent market. Have you had any interaction with fans over The Wraith?

FD: I can count on one hand those that were able to get in quickly and easily. It's certainly not the norm. They're often also the ones who burn their bridges just as quickly and are soon out of the business as fast as they entered it. The future of quality comic book storytelling lies in the independent market, but there's no money there and probably, generally speaking, never will be. The big publishers dominate the market and the distribution systems. They own it. And the indies can never compete with that. However, for those willing to search for better quality stories, there are plenty of indies out there producing some high quality stuff, but it can be hard to find, and it's hard to attract new readers when they don't know you're there.

I've had a great deal of interaction with fans over The Wraith, at conventions and via email, message boards etc. The vast majority of the reaction has been very positive and supportive, which has been most gratifying and humbling, particularly from those fans that really understand what we're trying to do with The Wraith.

APF: And what are you trying to do with The Wraith?

FD: Just tell the kinds of stories I grew up reading, a quality of story I think is lacking in the industry today. Solid, no nonsense storytelling without pretension, sans gimmicks and soap opera elements. A solid read of action, adventure, romance and a bit of melodrama thrown in.

APF: I've read everything I could on The Wraith so far and you've nailed it. Keep going.

I'm sure I'm not the only one looking forward to the new comics, the film and the new novel, *Valley of Evil.* If you had the chance to meet The Wraith and could ask only one question, what would it be?

FD: Thanks. I like to think we're doing our jobs well, and I intend to keep doing things well for as long as I can. One question? Hmm...I'd probably be too busy running away to think up some pithy question.

A.P. Fuchs is the author of several published novels, short stories and poetry. Among his most recent are *The Way of the Fog, Magic Man, A Red Dark Night* and *April,* a love story under the pseudonym, Peter Fox. He lives in Winnipeg, Manitoba with his wife and son. Visit him online at **www.apfuchs.com**

* Note: The following is the on-line journal entitled, *Lair Lines*, as it appeared on **www.the-wraith.com/movie** from February, 2004, to July, 2005. It has been lightly edited for this publication.

February 1 2004

I woke up today around 11 o'clock. Seem late? Not for a filmmaker. I was up late last night talking to Frank and working on my latest film, *A Good Place to Live*. I knew today would be a busy day, so I had to work out some last minute cuts before I went to bed. After I got up, I took my wife to work and came back home. I had to be at Derik's (producer) house at 1:30, so I had about an hour to kill. What did I do? I spent the hour with my son, who would end up spending the whole day with us. Derik and I were supposed to take some interior footage and basic "set-up" shots at his house, which is doubling for Leena's kitchen/bedroom and Latham's private study. We took pictures there while my son raised hell with Derik's little parrot-looking bird.

From there, Derik, my son, and I left and went downtown. Our city is very old, so a lot of the downtown district will fit the run-down areas of Metro City. We have a lot of great alleys and old buildings. We'll CGI tall skyscrapers and such into the actual film, but we took pictures of the "ground-level" buildings. This took a long while to shoot because of traffic and having to get out and unpack the equipment. We got more "establishing" shots and moved on from there.

Ryan, the actor playing The Cobra, was supposed to come along with another actor. The other guy was supposed to audition for the role of Latham, but due to a prior obligation to a local play, neither actor could make it.

This dented our schedule, mainly because we had to do a small shoot around 5 o'clock with Dietrich Adetayo (actor) for a pick-up shot on *A Good Place to Live*. I got myself a pizza and my son a Happy Meal and the three of us went back to my house to regroup. Derik and I planned out the next couple of weeks while I ate. We planned things out more and came up with details on our next shoot. Our next shoot will be solo scenes with Leena (Stacy Cooper). I can't really say much on the content of these scenes, however, pics will be available soon from the mentioned locations.

With 5 approaching, Dietrich made his presence known and came over to work on his pick-up shots. Last Tuesday was our original pick-up date, but because of snow, we had to delay it and sort of end one film and start another in the same day. This was very exhausting. We drove all over town catching footage for tie-in shots and scenery shots. We will be filming with actors very soon. Before the end of February, we plan on having around 3 scenes shot and completed. The first week of March will be a great week for us, and we hope to get around 6 done that week.

As we finished filming for *A Good Place to Live*, Dietrich came back to the studio and signed his contract for *The Wraith*. We're not sure where Dietrich will fall into *The Wraith*, but he'll be involved to some extent. Probably supplying us with the guns. I threw the footage we just shot into the mixer and gave them a rough cut of the film within minutes. After watching the cut, I kicked Dietrich's ass at a game of Halo for the Xbox. Both guys left and I went back to the editor.

Right now we're polishing off the film and getting it ready for viewing. As I toyed at the editor, I worked on more Wraith storyboards involving some of the footage we took. Then I remembered the Superbowl was on. I then remembered that I don't watch football, so I went back to work.

We're trying to achieve a certain look with the film, so today's shoot gave us the locations we need to get things rolling in the coming weeks. Next comes the lighting. I'll run by Derik ideas on the lighting and go over storyboards leading into the scenes with Leena.

I hope everyone enjoyed a recap of my day. It may sound like we didn't get much accomplished, but we're even more ready now to get this thing done for everyone. It takes a lot of time to make a film right, and we've always starting filming the locations first. It gives us a solid foundation to enter the characters into. I try to make all of my films atmospheric and "Sir Reel" to pull you into the characters. The way I see it, you gotta show your actors the world they'll be living in, so why not start there. I'll have a demo reel of locations to show them so they can get a feel for the shots to come.

Until next time...

Stephen J. Semones

February 21 2004

Ok, Frank promised a weekly, or close to it, journal entry, but I've been VERY busy as of late. I apologize to everyone wanting the latest Wraith film news. So, on to the latest from Sir Reel Films...

About a week ago I recieved our BRAND NEW 11x20ft green-screen. Chromakey certified for all photographic needs. Well, we needed one, so there you go. The company also sent me two peppermints and a pen for ordering a $200 screen. How nice, huh?
The same day, our Cobra contact lens arrived. It still remains in the vial it came in, but it looks like a weird science project. A couple of days later, I went out and purchased an 8 foot lighting rig with two 500 watt halogen bulbs in them. We can adjust the lights to almost any angle we need, and with our previous lighting system, look for *The Wraith* to have awesome lighting!!

The next thing on my list is a steadicam bar for the cameras and a pair of eyeglasses for the character Leena Patterson. I'll be getting these this week for sure. With the added equipment I just mentioned, I'd like to address another matter involving *The Wraith.*

Scott Leva. How cool is it to have this guy on board I ask? Very cool indeed. I loved X-Men, and to have Scott on board with *The Wraith* is spectacular. We decided to use some basic wire-work to spice up the action some, so expect top-notch delivery on this film all the way around the board!!!! I've been doing some storyboarding for Scott so we can kick everyone's ass with the fight scenes. They'll be simple in concept, but with Scott's know-how, we can take *The Wraith* to new levels professionally.

As mentioned earlier, I've been really busy. I've just finished the final print of *A Good Place to Live* and you can view it on my website. If you want to get a good idea for the lighting, camera style, and direction; check out this film!!!! *The Wraith* will be shot in similar fashion and style, but with more of a comic book/gothic-industrial feel to it. I'm very proud of *A Good Place to Live* and encourage everyone to see it.

Until Next Time...Be Cool, Be Loyal, Be There.

Stephen

February 29 2004

Ok, for a day that only comes around every four years, my "leap day" was by far strange but fulfilling. I got up today and got all our new equipment together and checked some email. After that, I began my day.

We were scheduled to shoot 3 (count them), 3 scenes today! We were going to do 3 Leena Patterson (Stacy Cooper) scenes, one which involved Michael Reeve (David Cooper). About 12:30, David calls me and tells me his wife is extremely ill with the stomach flu. We've all been there, so I totally understood. We were to begin filming around 5 anyway, so I had a few hours to work something up. I asked him if he would mind coming over and standing in front of the green-screen for a couple of reasons. We wanted some stills of David playing the undercover officer, Michael Reeve. Well, with no one else to shoot with, this was the next logical option. Publicity shots. We shot David in various poses standing in front of our green-screen.

We wanted to see how the screen looked, as this was the first time removing it from the package. We hit a snag. It's freaking huge people. With that much material, it becomes heavy and hard to hang with no rig (something we never thought of—can you believe it?). From being folded up for shipping, the screen is wrinkled. Well, it's going to be a few weeks before we actually need the screen, so we're going to order this wrinkle spray to straighten it out. This also gives us time to build a PVC structure to hold the huge screen. It's 20 feet tall by 11 feet wide, so PVC is the best option. Lightweight and portable.

Because we didn't get to film any actual scenes once again, we did plan out our re-shoot for this coming Wednesday, the day after our local release party for our last film, *A Good Place to Live*. We'll be resuming filming this Wednesday and again on Sunday. We're aiming for knocking out 5 scenes this week, and two next week. It's been a busy time for Team Wraith here in Tennessee, so bear with us. I sent Frank pics from our photoshoot, so he'll post a few of them I'm sure.

Another thing we tested today was a camera shot I'm inventing. It's something inspired from all of this bullet time crap we're seeing today. I've simplified the effect to cut around the subject very quickly, showcasing a different frame of action with each cut. In each shot you'll see a piece of the puzzle and as the cuts progress in a circular fashion around one subject. You'll see the whole picture and what's coming at you. It's not a morphing 360-degree-*Matrix* shot or a slow motion shot, but more of a very raw and energetic action sequence. As far as placement for the shot in the film, I can't divulge where it will go, but it will be very cool and unexpected.

We worked with David Cooper on the above shot today and will test it again soon. He really got into the character of Michael Reeve and was trying to develop every aspect of his personality, movements, and behavior today. His input on what it must be like to be Reeve was very intuitive and he grasped the ideology of becoming an undercover police officer. Though we don't go into much of the Reeve character in the film (as far as his job goes), it was good to see David covering all the basics today and putting on a show AS Michael Reeve.

As we approach our release party Tuesday, and our Wraith re-shoot on Wednesday, excitement fills the ranks of Sir Reel Films. Expect another journal update this week as well. I'll end on something actor David Cooper would like to say to all the Wraith fans and to Frank.

Until Next Time...

Stephen J. Semones

March 3 2004

Well, our release party last night went well. We had hoped for a bigger crowd, but we got the place half full at least. We had a blast and plugged the Wraith film several times. When *A Good Place to Live* was over and the credits started, the room was overwhelmed with applause. I was sure at that very moment that *The Wraith* will be something truly special. I also realized what I was put on this planet to do: Make films. It was a moment that defined my expectations from here on out. A moment that will stand forever with me as the beginning of it all.

We shot worked on three scenes tonight with the character Leena Patterson. We bagged one whole scene and worked on two more. One was a dream sequence which part of will be re-shot. I didn't like how it turned out, so Sunday we're re-shooting some of it. The third scene we shot involved the character Michael Reeve. About an hour into filming that scene, our mic went out. Well, we thought it was the mic anyways. We tested the mic on another camera and determined that the sound chip went bad in our camera. We took the camera to be fixed and it has to be sent off. That was our main camera, so yeah, we thought we were screwed.

I have a Mini DV camera, but no mic to plug in, so it renders that idea dead. It turns out we actually know someone who has a better camera than we did to start with and they're letting us use it until we get ours back. It's been bittersweet filming *The Wraith* so far. Things haven't gone as planned for the most part, but what we've been able to film thus far has been amazing, so I cannot complain one bit. Our shots with Leena are awesome in the scene we actually got completed. The rest of the stuff was good too; we just had some technical problems set us back a couple of days.

Our original plan was to wrap all three scenes today, but due to the camera messing up, we'll wrap those up on Sunday. As I see it, this puts us only around 1 week behind actual schedule, but what schedule am I on? We've decided to take as much time as needed to get each shot, each scene, each word spoken completely right!

I've also been working on concept designs for the Cobra costume and scepter, so we should see some Cobra pics surface fairly soon.

Expect a hit with *The Wraith* and keep the support strong!

Until Then...

Stephen

April 14 2004

A new blog will be added soon. In-the-meantime, we can announce today that actor Rick McVey, a stage actor from the world renowned Barter Theatre in Abingdon, Virginia, has come onboard as Robert Latham, the sinister crime lord who lives to one day bring down The Wraith.

More news shortly...

April 21 2004

Well today I woke up around 6:30 and worked my other job from 7 to 5. Quite a long day and then on to the filming. Several weeks ago we shot a couple of scenes, one of which included Michael Reeve and Leena Patterson waking up together before work. Well, I've been playing with that footage since then and have cut it together about 20 different ways and each one I pieced together seemed messy. Well, with David and Stacie Cooper's permission, we went back today and re-shot the entire scene. The scene lasts about 2-2 1/2 minutes and we took about 10 more takes.

Now, don't get me wrong, but even though the original shots we filmed for this scene were great, when it was pieced together, it seemed like it had too many cuts. The new version of the scene is done in one single take from beginning to end. No cuts at all. To get the shot of the two waking up together, I positioned a ladder in the corner of the bedroom set and rigged the tripod on. The tripod stuck out a good four feet, so it was dangerous trying to pan as we look down on the two characters the whole time, but fearless me decided to climb the ladder and risk broken parts of my anatomy to bring you all the best possible camera shot for the scene. Being the second full shoot we worked on this one scene, collectively we probably have two hours worth of takes equaling about 20-30 takes (roughly).

All I can say is that during today's re-shoot, David and Stacie gave it their all and got into character like nothing I've seen before. Either they were tired of shooting the scene over and over, or wanted deep down to make this the shot that we would use in the final cut of the film. Probably a little of both. Both actors poured their hearts into this scene and I believe that this will make a more solid opening for the characters in the film. Oh, did I mention that the first minute and a half of the scene that David Cooper acts as if he's listening to a news broadcast? Well, he had to memorize the newscast and act as if it were playing because we're adding that in during the post-production phase.

Well, to make a short story even longer, on the last take I fell off of the ladder and crashed to the floor below landing on my back. As I struck the floor, the camera rig on the ladder dropped down and using my ninja-like reflexes, I caught it before it smashed into a hundred pieces beside my head. I'm fine and thanks for asking, but luckily the camera was off and didn't get my poor imitation of Super Dave Osborne on film. However, I think I will be ridiculed from this day forth for my lack of coordination. It was worth it though and all done for The Wraith and our belief in Frank's comic. Luckily no one else has been injured yet and as things pick up, the safety will now be watched a lot closer. Leave it to the director to ruin all of the fun for the rest of the cast and crew :)
Well, after we packed up the equipment, we all sat down together and watched the dailies of the shoot and realized that this will be quite an enjoyable scene as it shows a great

sense of chemistry between David and Stacie. It should because they're really married, but it translates very well on camera and I know you all will not be disappointed.

Remember to stay tuned to this section of the site for all of the on-set news and mayhem as we bring you the best comic to film translation EVER!!!!!!!!

Until next time...

Stephen

April 25 2004

I know today isn't our normal day to film, but I had some extra time on my hands and wanted to get some behind the scenes stuff done for *The Wraith*. As you all may or may not already know, my mother agreed to do a voice over in *The Wraith*, portraying Leena's mother. My mom's best friend, Lisa Chandler, wanted to be involved as well, so I decided to see what we could get accomplished.

My whole life my mother (as most do) gave me direction. Today was payback. Haha! Seriously though, Lisa and my mother were open to the fact that as the director of *The Wraith*, I have obligations to see through. One of which is coming up with voice actors in a few scenes.

Around noon, my mother and her friend Lisa showed up with script in hand. They were both ready for the recording session, and to be as close to me as they are, they took my direction very well, and I didn't even have to get upset. We must have taken close to 30 takes with my mom and about 15 with Lisa. Before we recorded, we went over the dialogue, and they both offered suggestions as to how they should act this out. The weird thing is, neither of them have any voice acting experience, and they both did VERY WELL.

As many of you know, I have a studio in my house. Well, my wife took my son with her to run some errands and left the three of us here to pound out these recordings. It's all done digitally on my computer with a program called Wave Studio. Basically, I sat them both down and explained to them how to operate the program so they could do it at their own leisure and not feel pressured by me to produce on every take we did.

Sitting directly in front of the computer, they both had a reference script tacked up beside the monitor and recorded their parts into the microphone affixed to the top of the monitor. Sound easy? Guess again. To make it sound as if they were on an answering machine (which is what the script called for), I had to take a few measures to get the right sound quality. Number one, sound proofing the room. I closed the door and shoved a shirt underneath to reduce any outside noise. Number two I had to create the illusion of an answering machine message during playback. I turned on a ceiling fan to get a small hum, and mixed with the fan on the computer, it was a very straight forward sound compilation.

Some of you might think that this is very cheap and ineffective, but the rest of the sound quality I filtered through the program to get the desired effect. I added a small amount of echo and some white noise and it was done.

Being that this was the first time I've attempted such an elaborate task of recording someone's voice, I did prepare my mother and Lisa on what to expect from the scene they were voicing. I showed them both a rough edit and explained to them where their voices would come into play and the nature of what I expected. Both having read the script, they still needed that scene reference and were glad I was able to show them a rough cut of the scene for reference. To tell you how much they got into it, my mom even asked me to get her a prop phone so she could act it out a little better. WOW, I was impressed by their hard work and I'm sure everyone who sees the final cut of the film will be impressed as well.

Right now I'd publicly like to thank Frank for allowing me to cast my own mother and her best friend to voice these roles. Even though they are small parts, all the small parts add up to the overall picture, and I'm sure when Frank sees the scene, he'll love it. I'd also like to thank my mother and Lisa for taking the time to work with me on the recordings today and I'd like to recognize the hard work that they gave. They both gave 110% and it's this type of support that will make this film a success. My mother and Lisa are both photographers and will be doing a lot of the still photography for *The Wraith*, and their added involvement is much appreciated by all. It says a lot when your own family believes this much in your work and as a filmmaker it makes you believe that much more in your own project.

Until Next Time,

Stephen

May 24 2004

No new blog today from director Stephen Semones, I'm afraid to say, though one will be coming soon. I'd just like to announce here that we've signed Adam DiTroia to supply the film's music score, incorporating and elaborating the main theme (composed by legend Larry Groupé) into the film. Adam is a very talented musician who has worked in a myriad of mediums thus far (video games, films etc.), and we're extremely fortunate to have a man of his talent and experience onboard to create the kind of music score that we've always dreamed *The Wraith: Eyes of Judgment* of having. Welcome aboard, Adam :)

More news (and Stephen's latest blog) soon!

Frank Dirscherl
Executive Producer - *The Wraith: Eyes of Judgment*

June 6 2004

Today was one of the longest days of my life. I finished up Day 2 at the Adventure Con about 2 hours away from me and then came back to film with Rick McVey (Robert Latham) and David Semones (Charlie Grieco).

Last Sunday Derik Nutter and I set up the scene and walked through it several times planning out our camera shots and basically got everything ready for today's shoot. The scene we shot was the first scene that we see Latham and Grieco in the film and it originally called for the setting to be in Latham's office. Well after much consideration, we changed it slightly. Later on in the film The Cobra visits Latham in his office, so we wanted to show more of Latham's character, so we changed the setting from his office to his dinner table at home.

We planned a shoot from 6pm to 9pm and started filming around 6:30. We had a small contract signing session with Rick and David and then went right into filming. While they signed the contracts, Derik and I set up the cameras and lights. After they were finished with the contracts, Derik and I were still setting up, so Rick and David decided to walk through the scene several times and get into character. Then it was time to film.

When we worked on our last film, *A Good Place to Live*, we would literally do like 10 takes and out of those we would probably be able to use only 1 or 2. Tonight Rick and David were so prepared and into character that they nailed the scene on the very first take. As the director, I knew that only one take would be a stupid move to make, so I kept taking more. Every 2 or 3 takes I would change the camera placement slightly. We ended up with about twenty or more takes and there were only 4 that I had to call "cut" on. These guys took their parts so serious and got into their characters so well that I sat there thinking that we are honestly creating history! We are literally changing the way Independent films will be shot and it was exciting, to say the very least.

This was the first time that I had worked with Rick and his acting was brilliant. He brought so much to the table as Robert Latham that now I can't see anyone else playing the part. EVER. David, which some of you may or may not know, is my brother. He has done the music for four of our films thus far and this makes his third acting role we have given him. Now I will admit that David wasn't my original choice for the role of Charlie Grieco, but with Derik pulling for him, I caved in and gave him the shot. The reason I wasn't too keen on him playing Grieco was that he hasn't tried anything that deep before, but now I'm glad I listened to Derik. David IS Charlie Grieco now!! He came in and acted so professionally that I couldn't believe my own eyes. He had such good chemistry with Rick that now I can't see anyone else doing these parts. They both had me believing that they hated The Wraith and I sat there completely spellbound by their acting.

After we finished filming, I shot a little bit of improv stuff for the upcoming trailer; that went extremely well too. I also took some stills of them and we wrapped up shooting on schedule at 9pm. If we were doing a Hollywood production, we would have probably spent 12 hours shooting this scene and we did it in a little less than 3. That's how good these two guys did and I can't wait for everyone to see it now. I'm sending Frank some stills today, so expect the Downloads gallery to be updated very shortly. You'll also get to see a few shots that we did in the upcoming trailer.

I bought a brand new 3 chip Mini-Dv camera this week and we used it for the first time tonight. Let me tell you that I can't believe the quality of this scene. It is almost film quality and we used very little lighting in the scene. I attached a wide angle lens because we were shooting in a small room and it literally makes the room look HUGE!!!!!! You now will get to see Latham at home looking over his business reports and having wine with dinner and it looks amazing. This has to be the most fun I've had shooting in a very long time (possibly ever) and it's mainly because of Rick and David. These guys will impress you when you see the film, because their acting is top notch and they are so into their roles that it's totally believable.

I can't wait for you all to see this film now. Look for another Lair Line next week!

Until Then...

Stephen

June 15 2004

Well, today was a strange one to say the least. We're not even through with the film and we've went back to do pick up shots. Well, let me explain...

I purchased a new camera and received it a little over a week ago. It's a higher-end model than what we were using, so knowing that we weren't too far into filming and we're still waiting on The Wraith costume, I decided to re-shoot a scene that we've already bagged. The reason is to get the same quality that we achieved last week. I decided to change the angles on this scene once more and come up with some new techniques for the scene.

We scheduled a 7pm start time with David (The Wraith) and Stacie (Leena) Cooper. They arrived and for about 30 minutes I went over their new contracts with them. For the next hour we rehearsed and walked through this scene and how we planned on shooting it with the actors. Around 8 pm, my mother Janet showed up to do the still photography. Jim Taylor and Marc Kimball both had requested some special pictures to be taken, so after filming we shot those as we had promised them.

It was a stressful night for several reasons. Once we got rolling we got a lot of good takes, but getting rolling was the hard part. David and Stacie had basically forgotten this scene and moved on to the rest of the script and going back was a headache. They had already shot this scene on two separate occasions in the past, so I was thinking the third time's a charm. I had gotten to the set an hour before the cast to set everything up and once we were ready to shoot, I realized we needed to adjust the lights. 30 minutes later I was still trying to get the lighting right as everyone started to grow hungry and impatient. Once the lights were situated we walked through the scene several times so David and Stacie would know their marks. The new way we were shooting this scene was breaking it down into three separate cuts. First a wide shot establishing the setting and cast, then cutting to a close up side angle getting the bulk of the dialogue, and going back to a wide shot to finish the scene. Sound easy? Think again. We had to shoot the beginning, ending, and middle in that order and it made it more difficult to get the lines and marks right. I guess it was my fault for being so damn insistent on shooting this way, thus making it hard on everyone in the process. Don't get me wrong, the takes were good but very trying on the cast and crew.

After several takes we took a break and gathered our thoughts. After the break the shoot went so smoothly and fast. We ended up wrapping for the day around 11pm, so not too bad a shoot as far as time goes. I have to hand it to David and Stacie for trusting in me to get this scene shot right because I know they were getting aggravated doing this a third time. They are doing so well and I know it has to be irritating to go back and do something over that was right the first two times. Well, the second time at least. The first time we shot this scene it was so cut up with takes it would literally have 13 cuts or shots when the scene was edited. The second time we did it in one whole cut, and tonight we got it in three cuts. I think this new version of the scene is the best overall and will work the best once we go into editing.

Right now I'd just like to thank everyone involved with this film both cast and crew who believe in *The Wraith*, the script, and me as the director. It means so much to have such a dedicated group of people working together on this and I know it will be worth it once it's completed. In fact, I guess it's my job to decide what needs to be re-shot, but I know sometimes I let the creative side get the best of me. Thanks guys for working with me so hard on this film!! You deserve more than you know for your efforts. Thanks also goes to the people who sit by and anticipate this film and look forward to seeing it completed. Next week is Father's Day, so the cast and crew have the day off, but I'll be working on editing so expect a new Lair Line the following weekend.

Until then, have a happy Father's Day everyone!!!!!!!!!

Stephen

<u>July 12 2004</u>

Today went well and I had a lot of fun. I got to play a drunken bum in the film and have a crucial part in part of the story arc. I got to give the undercover officer Reeve The Wraith mask that was found in an alley.

As a director it's hard to act as well, and I'm no actor, so I'm apologizing to everyone now before you see the film. Hopefully with the magic of editing and a musical score, we can beef up my performance.

It was extremely hot today, so as a bum, I had quite a bit of clothing on. My teeth were blacked out; I had dirt all over my face as well as almost a week without shaving. I had about 2 layers of clothes on and to top it off, I had a crushed/half-burned cigarette hanging out of my mouth and a liquor bottle in my hand. I was quite the bum. No seriously. I think I really pulled off the look well.

Today started with meeting up with Derik Nutter about 1:00 and from there we had to make one last call before the shoot. We couldn't decide on one location to shoot the scene. We had two places scouted and had to make a last minute call. It was a better choice in the end, well except for giant air cooling units turning on every 20 minutes giving us a small shooting window in intervals. At one point a leaf blower nearby started up and people were shouting and interfered with a take, so after 15 minutes filming, 20 minutes waiting to start back, 15 more minutes of filming, etc., we decided it was going to be a long and very hot day.

Derik and I met David Cooper at the park so he could follow us to the set. Ty Kelsey (producer) and Zek Hensely (Storyboard Artist) showed up to accompany us. Rolling in last was Best Friends Photos to do the stills for the day. We made it to the set about 15 minutes after 2. Cooper and I rehearsed some more for our Oscar Winning Scene while Derik, Ty, and Zek set up the cameras. Then it was time to do a walkthrough before we rolled cameras.

When we walk through a scene before filming, we use storyboards if we have them and a script and do several dry runs to get the flow of the scene down. This helps the actors in the scene know where the cameras will be as well as their marks. We shot for about three hours and called it a day. We had enough footage to take to the editing bay. It was very easy working with Cooper in this scene. I can tell that he's matured as an actor and the ideas he had to help make the scene even better were outstanding. David came up with so many good ideas that most will be incorporated in the final film. For instance, David played off the fact that I was a bum and probably smelled, so in one take he stepped back from me and waved the odor from his face. Sheer brilliance on his part!!!!! It's the little things like that one that helps make the film better. It shows you how much the actors get into their roles and want to make the film better.

When we wrapped I felt as if I had lost several pounds in the hot sun with the clothing on. Oh well, I could stand to loose a few pounds, and it doesn't bother me one bit because it was all for The Wraith.

Until Next Time...

Stephen

<u>July 18 2004</u>

Well, I got up knowing that today would be a very long day. Knowing this, I decided to clean house the day before and straighten up because I knew what the day would hold for us at Sir Reel Films.

Lance and Jeremy from Xtreme Design FX drove four hours from South Carolina to hand deliver to us The Wraith costume. Before I get into all the costume stuff, let me just say that these guys have XTREME talent and when I finally got to meet them in person, I understood more of what went into making one of these costumes and what Hell we put them through to do the suit for us.

Jeremy called me about 9:45pm and told me where he was and asked how to find where I lived. Well, after figuring out they were on the wrong side of town, I hopped in the car with Producer Ty Kelsey and rushed to their location. Once there Jeremy got out of the car, followed by Lance, and introduced himself. After a brief introduction, we left the ghetto and drove five minutes to my place. No, I don't live in the ghetto, but close. :)

Well, once they brought the costume in, we proceeded to get the actor and Wraith himself into the costume. You'll get to see some of this stuff on our next web documentary by the way. Anyways, when you wear a suit like this naturally you'll get hot and sweaty, so we had to powder up David's legs before he could even get into the legging. The suit is basically one main piece and he puts it on starting at his legs, then sticks his arms in bringing it onto his body, then we zip him up in the back. It takes 2 to 3 people besides himself, just to get him into this suit. After he's wearing the main piece, then we slide on the boots, gloves/gauntlets, apply the belt, and then the cowl.

David walks back downstairs to where everyone was waiting. Upon seeing him everyone was silent for a moment taking in this awesome site. He looked so real and natural as The Wraith, at that moment everything we had hoped for this film in the last 10 months fell into place. We tested out his movement and realized that he'll basically have NO limitations in the suit, although it is extremely hot and weighs roughly around 15 pounds. Having never met David before, even to do a body cast for the suit's mold; Xtreme Design got the suit almost completely perfect based on pictures they had seen and his measurements alone. The cape was the perfect length, his suit fit perfectly, and the cowl fit him like a glove. No worries here, Lance, this thing is perfect. Great job!! The only adjustment that they made to the suit was trimming the neck of the costume. The neck piece was just a little too tall for David's face, but it still fit him when he first put it on. He could tell that after wearing the suit for a while, that piece may scrape his neck, so the next thing I know, Jeremy and Lance have the suit in the floor cutting it down to size. How cool is that???? They fixed the only problem (and it wasn't really a problem!!) right there on the spot.

Jeremy and Lance brought their wives with them, and we should talk about them briefly. You can tell that these two guys are happy with what they do for a living because their significant others came and showed their support for the venture. Come to find out, one of them even works on the "weathering" process of costume making. They all pour their heart into their works and it shows by how dedicated they were in making sure that this costume was of the highest possible durability and appearance. Because they don't normally make superhero costumes just for a movie, they had to make alterations to the normal costuming process, which is why it took a while to get done. It's just the four of them doing the whole process and most feature films have an endless supply of people at their disposal. They had to modify the costume to take the pressure of being the only costume in the film, which most feature films have an endless supply of them, and still making it look like the comic and not cheesy for the film version. Well, they succeeded beyond what I expected and everyone who sees the film will not realize the hard work, dedication, and talent that went into sculpting and creating this costume. These guys deserve more than what they got on this costume, so the least I can do is tell them how great a job they did on the suit and let them know that this is the beginning of a wonderful relationship between Sir Reel and Xtreme. The costume, simply put, is an artistic masterpiece.

I asked Jeremy about how many hours it took to do the costume. He laughed and then said countless. He then told me that the hardest part of the whole thing was probably getting the chest piece right. I saw just a small portion of what they did and I have the most respect for costume designers as I possibly can. They poured so much creative thinking into the suit, just to get it exactly the way it had to be for the film and how it looks in the comic.

Well, after talking to them, taking pictures and footage of their visit, we had to say goodbye. They had decided to stay at a local hotel for the evening and drive back the next day. Their next project was a Flash costume. I can't wait to see that. Overall, the costume will work perfectly for bringing the Dread Avenger of the Underworld to life and delivering the best comic adaptation ever!!!!!!! Well, except for Spider-Man, but I don't exactly have a $100 million dollar budget do I????

Until Next Time...

Stephen

July 22 2004

Well, this won't be your traditionally long and winded Lair Line that I usually deliver. Ok, maybe not, but I'll try. I've had a long day, working 10 hours at my "real" job and then basically driving across town to the set to film for close to 5 more.

After a brief detour to my house to pick up all the cameras, lights, and Wraith costume, I realized that on the way to the set, an overwhelming string of phone calls concluded that my crew couldn't make it for this or that reason. Screw 'em. I'm making a movie here, with or without a crew. So I arrive at the set, which is actually the star of the film's house, David Cooper. Dave and I unpack it all, and I mean all of it. "Where's the crew?" he asked. "I'm the crew," I replied. After about 20 minutes of unchained laughter from Dave, I convinced him I was serious and would be shooting it myself.

The very first film I made had 2 people that made it. David and I. That's it and the memories were coming back, and seeing how far we progressed, we decided to do this one right. From *Trippin' Nuts! The Movie* to *The Wraith*, we had come so far and no crew might mean a good thing. There was one dilemma. David can't play two parts at the same time. Someone needed to play The Wraith, and that someone apparently had to be me.

The scene called for The Wraith to visit Michael Reeve at his apartment. I won't spoil you and go into details, but anytime the shot called for both characters to be onscreen at once, we had to improvise. Now doing this all the time can really bring down the quality of the film, but sometimes it's more intimate and personal. I had to direct, run the camera, and wear the gauntlets for the same scene. Believe it or not, you would think we had a full crew working in this scene. The whole scene wasn't filmed this way of course, but for most of the end of the scene, it is.

We watched the footage on the spot to basically see if we could pull this off and make it look good, and guess what...WE DID. Anyone watching the film and hasn't read this Lair Line, WILL NOT be able to tell the difference at all. Coop and I have such a long friendship and work history, we know what the other is thinking and it makes all the difference when you're in a bind like we were. As dedicated as we were to the film, we felt we owed it to ourselves to attempt the nearly impossible and see what the outcome would be. Worst case scenario: we have to re-shoot and call it a day.

We took probably close to an hour worth of footage and I got some great shots to work with later in post. As hard as tonight's shoot went, it was worth it overall. Not everyone will realize the hard work that went into making this film and that's why I talk about it here. No one ever said making one was easy, but most of the time it's not like tonight. We got down to our filmmaking basics and it paid off. Put us in our place and made us realize more than we did that we all have to help ourselves and sometimes two men in a war trench is better than six.

Well, enough about the trials of filmmaking. Needless to say, we did what we set out to do, and it took us a while longer, but who cares? We got what we needed and it's good. This is actually a crucial scene in the film, so I'll have some pictures circling around soon. I hope everyone likes what they've seen from us in the last month or so, and I hope everyone checks out the newest documentary we released. The first trailer was delayed a bit, but should be ready in around a month. I started editing on it yesterday, so look for it soon!!!!!

Until Next Time...

Stephen

August 14 2004

BRISTOL, TN. - Once again Sir Reel Films have outdone themselves, but this time it's a whole new medium. Sir Reel Films would like to proudly announce that they have secured the clearance to have the world premiere of *The Wraith: Eyes of Judgment* at the world famous Abingdon Cinemall Theater.

The Cinemall is one of three George Lucas-approved theaters in the entire US. It boasts itself as the only theater on the eastern seaboard to have people from over 42 states and 3 countries to visit for the premiere of *Star Wars: Episode 2*. Each theater has a 65 speaker digital surround sound system, stadium seating, and they carry custom made projectors with special Zenon bulbs that produce a picture that's over 100% brighter than your average theater. They have been showcased on ABC's *Good Morning America* show and designated as the best movie theater in the USA by both news media and local patrons.

Please visit the Cinemall website at: www.cinemall.com for more information on the theater.

The premiere of the film will be sometime in March or April of 2005 and will have a short run at the Cinemall before going off to festivals and conventions. Expect the entire cast and crew on hand for pictures, autographs, and more as the Cinemall hosts the release party for the media and local patrons.

Sir Reel Films are extremely honored to be able to have the public view this film on such a big level and are looking forward to showing for the first time at the Abingdon Cinemall. What better place to show the best Independent Comic Book Film of all time? There isn't a better place.

Thank you.

August 21 2004

Ok, it's been since July 22 since you guys got a proper new Lair Line from me and I'm about to tell all you Wraithheads why!!!

Well, we released a trailer? Have you seen it yet? If not, please check it out. As you may or may not know, it IS a teaser and does its job. Trust me, you'll all get a glimpse of The Wraith in action fairly soon, but don't expect too much too soon now. :)

After releasing the trailer, I secured us a deal to premiere this film at the world-famous Cinemall. This is a VERY big deal because this theater is state of the art. George Lucas himself has stamped his approval on this theater and they are not too proud to tell you so. This theater has 65 speakers in each theater, including a giant water-cooled subwoofer. This place is really insane and I can't think of anyplace better to premiere *The Wraith*. They use custom made projectors that are 100% brighter than a regular screen. Because we're filming this in mini DV, the picture quality will be top notch and accompanied dearly by the 5.1 sound mix being supplied by Voodoo Studios. Check out the Cinemall here: www.cinemall.com and try to come to the premiere.

While playing Mr. Bigshot (LOL) and securing those deals, I've also been preparing to shoot with Mandi Leigh September 4th & 5th. We're flying her in that weekend from LA and pulling her from her busy schedule to shoot a scene in the film. During that weekend, I'll also be directing her music video that will be on the DVD and released on the Internet sometime between now and the next couple of months. In fact, right now it's about 2:20am. I have to be at work in less than six hours and after 10 hours of that, I'll be planning Mandi's scene shot by shot on location with Derik Nutter and then rehearsing it with the actors. I then have to be at work at 5am Monday morning and work 10 more hours, thus repeating the cycle of killing myself all the way around. However I'm not complaining one bit. I have a fairly easy job and I'd work even harder to get this film made. I'm basically telling you all that I'm basically working 24 hours a day to get this film made as well as providing for my family. All the hard work is finally paying off with a successful trailer release and a premiere location and after it's shot only will I rest. Hahaha. I turned 27 this past Thursday and I guess I'm trying to do it now while I'm young. I've also been dwelling a lot on my age lately, and I can honestly say that if I would have tried doing this film 6 years ago I would have failed. I've been making films since I was 19 and I'm still learning and this has been the best experience yet!!!

Last Sunday I shot some pickup shots of David in his Wraith costume as well as bagged a scene with Stacie Cooper. The pickup shots were basically for a scene we previously worked on that required him to be in the suit, but the first time the lighting wasn't as good as it should have been. We basically knew what we wanted and got it in like 15 minutes from having to do it once before. The Leena scene we also worked on turned out very good too! I've been developing a new camera technique and proved my theory correct in that scene. Also for that scene we used something for the very first time. A neutral density lens filter. We lit her scene up too good and had neon white walls all around her, so on went this new filter and WOW!!!! It sucked all the bad light straight out of there and gave it a wonderful clarity. I'll be using this thing often now. Hehehe... The camera technique is something I kind of invented one day and tried, but realized it needed some refinement. Having forgotten my steadi-cam attachment, I decided to try something. New filmmakers pay attention here because I'm about to teach you something cool. I wanted an overhead shot of Leena as she was sitting down and wanted the camera to go from overhead to pan down in front of her and go down to the floor angling up. Ok, I extended two tripod legs the entire length and left one about halfway. Then I slid two of the legs beside of me at my hips and put the shorter leg firmly against my chest. Angling the view screen on the camera down I could monitor the whole shot and move the tripod with my body, thus steadi-camming the shot!!! It moved fluidly like a steadi-cam, but I could get a better angle with it. After about 3 tries, I had it down and got a VERY cool shot. Ok, class is dismissed.

As filming progresses on *The Wraith*, you'll probably hear less and less from me as far as Lair Lines go, but I will still do them when I can. I was going to do one last Sunday and forgot. From now until Mandi gets here, we won't be shooting. We're rehearsing everything down to the last detail and camera shot, so expect a BIG Lair Line as well as several new pictures in the following days of that shoot!!!!!!

Until Next Time...Take Care and God Bless!!

Stephen

<u>September 7 2004</u>

"I have something to do before the end. I must see it through, sir, if you understand."
- J.R.R. Tolkien

That is a quote I now live by. This weekend was by far one of the best, if not the best, experience I've ever had making a film. Mandi Leigh came in Saturday the 4th and was with us for two days. We shot a scene for the film with her both nights and during the day worked on a music video for the song "Home of Darkness." The music video is being edited now and will be on *The Wraith* DVD.

Before I continue, I'd like to personally address Mandi Leigh. It was an honor to shoot her music video and a pleasure having her in this film. Mandi was an absolute joy to work with both personally and professionally. I've never done a music video before and she worked so hard with me to make it a success, and I guarantee that it will be. Mandi is such a beautiful and talented individual and I know she is going to go very far. It was a wonderful experience having her here for the weekend and I hope I get to work with her again soon. I shot a small video diary for her fans that should be available soon at www.mandileigh.com You'll get to see some clips from her scene in the film and music video as well as the usual Sir Reel hilarity.

We shot the music video in a warehouse putting Mandi in front of 2 greenscreens. We have a 20-foot-tall by 11-foot wide greenscreen that she was standing in front of with a 9-foot-tall by 6-foot-wide one to her left boxing her in. It took us a while to get the lighting right, but once we did, we were ready to roll and Mandi sang her heart out for us. We worked in front of the greenscreen most of Saturday and Sunday afternoon. The last thing we shot for the video was on the actual film location. It all turned out very well and I can't wait for everyone to see it.

The film shoot both nights went very well. We had some slight casting issues that we had arise at the very last minute, but thanks to a loyal friend and Sir Reel follower, we replaced someone last minute and everything worked out fine. Once again, Mandi was very cool to work with, and this being her first actual speaking role on film, she was very patient and allowed us to do our thing. I say patient because on film sets there are ALWAYS delays and we had our share, but we worked through it and everyone's patience paid off. The last thing we did Sunday night was watch both daily reels and everyone was happy at the end of the weekend, so that's all that mattered.

The film shoots were grueling because of the nature of the scene. It's a fight scene, and we had dialogue, plus multiple angles to get. Lighting was an issue at first, but we worked through that. Let me stop and say this: Lighting an entire alley way evenly for each shot is not easy and should not be attempted unless you're willing to waste an hour of time each night blending light for each shot. We did it, but it was cumbersome and tiring. Overall, everything matches up VERY well and I'm pleased with how everything has turned out. The actual fight isn't that long, but by blending angles and shots and timing some things when I edit, this will look extremely cool!!! I will however state that the set got a little bloody, so take that for what it's worth ;)

Also, Sir Reel films is like a fellowship. The Fellowship of the Wraith. LOL I want to personally thank everyone who was involved this weekend with the long shoots. Everyone banded together to make this the best damn shoot we could and we pulled it off with ease. Everyone believes in *The Wraith* and what this film means. When I was on set Sunday afternoon I looked around and saw all these people working together, including Mandi and I, I almost got all emotional. The whole cast and crew were all busting their asses and working hard to make sure this project is top notch. The level of enthusiasm and dedication to this film is overwhelming. Thank you everyone who worked this weekend. Thank you for making this a truly wonderful experience. Mandi, Ryan, Cooper, Randy, Zek, Derik, Ty, Blake, Janet, Lisa, Christie, and Frank (who was there in spirit)....Thank you all for the hard work and dedication.

Expect in the coming weeks a couple of new web documentaries, the "Home of Darkness" video, a new trailer, Mandi's video diary, and plenty of pictures. I hope you all enjoy.

Until Next Time...

Stephen

A Video Diary featuring a look at the shooting of Mandi Leigh's superb music video for the love song from *The Wraith*, "Home of Darkness" has been added to the Documentaries section of the site. Don't dare miss it! We're so thankful and blessed to Mandi and her team for participating in making *The Wraith: Eyes of Judgment* all it can be, and rest assured it's people like them, committed to excellence, that stir us on to even greater heights :)

Here's also your first look at our first teaser, prelim movie poster. We'll have a few variants appearing over the months, before the final version you'll see at the Cinemall (for our cinematic premiere) and on video/DVD boxes. But for now, check this out...

Frank

October 20 2004

Well, it's been a little over a month since you got a Lair Line from me, and I'm sorry. I finished editing the video for "Home of Darkness," and right now it's in the hands of Alex Riback (editor) who's currently working on the chromakey in the video. The video is going to be completely awesome and I can't wait to unveil it on the world.

Today we shot quite a bit at a local motel here in town. We were shooting various Cobra shots (the first time cameras have rolled on this character so far!) and actually got something like five different scenes done and bagged. Ryan Basham is great as always and a pleasure to work with. He brings so much diversity to The Cobra character, and I'm hoping everyone loves his performance. He's done his villain research and it will show. He's a natural actor and I can't say enough good things about him. Anyway, Ryan totally got into his character and blew us away.

Because of Derik Nutters unfortunate accident a week or so back, he was unable to be with us this week. He was here in spirit and he is taking some time off to recover so he can come back stress free. In his place, Ty Kelsey stepped up to the plate with his new Assistant Director promotion and worked very close with me to ensure all bases were covered. Ty has a great mind for what looks and feels good in a scene and it's a blessing having him on set. By the time we started rolling cameras it was well after 8pm and probably getting close to 9. We wrapped at 1am and left the motel feeling like we had a productive evening.

Two fellow co-workers of mine stopped by because they are HUGE fans of ours and wanted to see some filming in action. After a few takes, they as fans immediately started giving us input based on what we were already shooting. Since this is aimed towards The Wraith fans, listening to these two was a great help and inspired Ty, Ryan, and myself as to why we're making this film. It may not be the best film, but it will be well worth watching just to see how much collaboration went into its making. Having some outside input and advice seemed to push us to succeed for the fans and not just ourselves. So, believe it when we say, this film is for everyone. It's for the fans and the soon to be fans.
The actual filming went very well. With Derik out indefinitely, Ty and I had to really push Ryan to get these scenes done so we would not fall farther behind and so we could get as much done in one night without having to rent a motel room again. Needless to say, the room got semi-trashed as an air unit and smoke detector fell apart (with some tinkering of course) and I believe a couple of phones got thrown around, but hey, it's all for the good of the film.

Due to a prop issue, part of the Cobra origin has been slightly modified to fit, but what we have now actually adds a little more mysticism to The Cobra character and doesn't spoil everything in the scene like it originally did. We trimmed it down slightly to allow the end of the film to have a little more shock value. I think everyone will be impressed and will love Ryan's interpretation of The Cobra. He may not look exactly like the character from the comic, but he's close enough. Some minor modifications were made to allow Ryan to portray him and it be believable, but believable is how he comes across and I swear you all will love the transformation that takes place.

Well, I'm extremely tired now and need to catch up on some sleep. Look for some stills from the motel. The "Home of Darkness" music video is aiming for a December release, but it depends on how long the post production FX will take, so please bear with us. When the video is released, all I will say is that YOU WILL see The Wraith in action as well as other shots never seen before from the film. I look forward to showing you guys really soon, so be patient and good things will come. I guarantee it!

Until Next Time...

Stephen

<u>October 27 2004</u>

What a great night of filmmaking we had last weekend. It's been a hectic week and our shoot was a good way to cap off the week before a relaxing day off. Finally. However, I'll spend most of it compiling Wraith footage, but hey, I enjoy it and it relaxes me.

Last weekend's filming session was to have been the shooting of three separate scenes, but we only were able to get to two. Stacie Cooper was unable to make the shoot, so we dropped that scene and focused on the other two instead. We'll be able to pick up that scene later, but I was happy just to have been behind the camera.

The two scenes we shot were kind of odd in comparison to shoot in one night. One was a very small scene in The Wraith car between Max Horton and The Wraith himself. Not THE WRAITH CAR, but the one in the film. Actually the car is my new '04 Mitsubishi Outlander that has a similar body style to the one in the comic. Neat, huh? I know, I know. Enough about the car. Ok, this was the first time so far that Nathan Blevins has got to shoot any scenes as Max. Being real good friends with David Cooper himself, Nathan was able to just sink right into Max and bring him from page to screen with ease. The Irish accent was great and he has such charisma that it's really a joy to work with him. Nathan is so laid back and reserved that his acting style just takes you completely off guard.

The scene we shot just before that was with Robert Latham and his right hand man Charlie aka Rick McVey and David Semones. The scene we shot was not in the original script and I'll explain why. When discussing ideas for the DVD with Frank, I had an idea to give more character scenes as bonus footage. Rick had been idle for a while and I wanted to work with him again. What I decided to do was flesh out an outline script and give some key ideas I wanted to present and let them have at it. The result of this improv hybrid method of filmmaking was strictly brilliant. Not on my part, but Rick and David's. They pulled out all the stops and delivered two of the best performances I think I've ever seen either of them do. They were totally with it in this scene. I'd like to add this scene into the actual film as their introduction scene, but if it doesn't make it there, it will definitely be on the DVD. We'll see how Frank likes it and go from there. If it doesn't make the final cut, ah well, everyone will still get to see this awesome villain scene.

Working with Rick and my brother David is always a pleasure and honor. Their chemistry is so good onscreen and offscreen that I can't wait to shoot more with them. Today also marked the first day that actor Nathan Blevins worked as a Talent Coach on the film. His job: assist the other actors with dialogue and body language techniques and suggestions. Nathan is a great stage actor and will really help bring the best out of our already stellar cast!!!! Everyone has really pulled together lately to help make this the best film possible and I can't wait to show everyone exactly how hard we've all worked.

I have plenty of pictures and a new interview/web documentary coming your way this week!!! Also, there should be a second trailer by Christmas, so everyone keep a look out. Expect this to be a full length trailer with completed footage and shots of The Wraith in action!!!! Also Mandi Leigh has asked me to direct another music video for her song called "Provocative." I would personally like to thank her for the opportunity and look forward to working with this very talented gal again soon. It has been my privilege and honor to work with everyone involved in this film so far and would like to thank everyone for all their hard work.

Until Next Time...Peace!

Stephen

<u>November 9 2004</u>

Bear with me; I'm going on very little sleep. We re-visited Rick McVey's (Robert Latham) office building to do a small shoot involving the Leena, Paul, and Max characters. The scene turned out very, very well.

I guess what caught my eye about this location was the checkered tile floor. Actually an office building, this hallway was converted into an apartment building hallway for the scene. The scene is basically this—Leena comes out of Michael Reeve's apartment and sees someone at the end of the hall. Very little dialogue, but the scenery is awesome in this scene.

The hallway was long enough for us to do a Stanley Kubrick shot. Rick was kind enough to lend us his dolly so we could pull it in front of Stacie (Leena) as she came down the hall. I tried it several ways standing on it while Zek Hensley pulled me down the hall, but I found the best shot overall (and the one I want in the final cut) by accident. Holding camera equipment any length of time will tire your arms. I was already tired and stretching after holding my arms up in the air. I held the camera up over my head and as I was stretching my neck, I looked up and found my shot on the camera monitor.

When you see the shot onscreen, it will appear as if the camera is on a track that is mounted on the ceiling aiming down at Leena as she comes down the hallway. At the end of the hall, the camera drops down as she runs offscreen. Very cool shot. I highly recommend a dolly for people just starting out and they are not hard to build or acquire. I've used one before on *A Good Place to Live*, but unless the shot really needs a dolly, then I don't usually like to use one.

Tonight I got to work with Nathan Blevins, Stacie Cooper, and David Cooper. Once again, it was my complete pleasure to work with these guys again. Stacie and Nathan did exceptionally well and I would mention David's role (which was done very well, too), but don't want to spoil the film for you. This is a pivotal scene in the film, and albeit short, the scene was shot perfectly and this will be one of those scenes that stand out.

Every actor on this film is giving absolutely one-hundred percent that they have to bring you the best possible film we can deliver. They've all matured as actors on this film and it will show in comparison to our earlier works. This has been a great learning experience for everyone, and hey, this is only the beginning of it all.

Until Next Time...

Stephen

December 6 2004

First off I'd like to say Happy Birthday today to my Dad. His birthday is today and I missed seeing him today, but I gave him a card yesterday and will see him tomorrow. Sorry I couldn't swing by today. Happy Birthday Dad!! Love ya man! ;)

Today was VERY crazy indeed. I have a confession to make. I'm an addict. I've been playing Halo 2 every spare moment I can and chose to play it last night instead of going straight to bed. I had to work from 7 to 3 today at my paying job, which meant I got about three hours sleep. You all could care less, but as soon as I got off work, I headed straight to the warehouse for the remainder of our shoot. Being the Director and all, I couldn't make the first hour of the shoot because of work, but I got there as quick as I could. Luckily Assistant Director Ty Kelsey was there to get the ball rolling in my brief absence.

My son (he's four by the way) and I went to the warehouse yesterday to get the set ready. En route with us was The Wraith costume, makeup, lights, 2 green screens, fog machine (never leave without this baby!), power cords, etc. Needless to say, my car was filled to the brim yesterday. The warehouse is about a thirty to forty minute drive from here, so after twice yesterday and twice today, I AM TIRED.

I got there just before four o'clock because we thought I had left Leena's glasses at my house. After detouring back and forth for a minute (including changing clothes while driving), I finally made my way to the warehouse. The glasses were already there waiting. When I arrived Tyrell was pacing frantically back and forth trying to set up shots while Zek Hensley helped him. Stacie Cooper was walking around rehearsing lines and reading over the scenes. Nathan Blevins was applying theatrical makeup to "age" himself for the Max role, and David Cooper, The Wraith himself, was walking around in costume just hanging out. We began filming after a few short minutes and realized Nathan had to leave shortly to go to his paying job. We only had like thirty minutes to get all of his shots done, which wasn't going to be easy. Because of the rehearsal time and el cheapo storyboards I drew in my script, the cast was ready and nailed it within a few takes. Awesome job from these guys!!!

We wrapped around 9pm and headed back home. Car full of equipment plus the whole cast and crew poked up the road to finish the day unloading the vehicle at my house. I must say, I really enjoy filmmaking at this level. Though I dream of having a studio backing us, right now the whole independence factor really makes it worthwhile. While filming tonight I noticed how much the cast and crew go back and forth over the dialogue and camera shots. I was faced tonight with a lot of input from everyone and it paid off. It made a crucial scene in the film that much better. Just little character mannerisms these guys add bring soooo much depth to the film. If this were a BIG studio production, we wouldn't be able to work a scene out like we did without some committee poking their noses in.

As of today we stand at about 80% complete shooting the film. This doesn't count for re-shoots or post production, so overall completion on the film is right about 60%. Not much but not bad either. If you do the math, most of the work to do now is in post production. Hopefully by February we'll be done shooting and the film will have already hit post. I am really pleased with how far everyone has come on this film and look forward to showcasing it to the world.

Until Next Time...

Stephen

January 31 2005

Well, we're getting closer. Closer to finishing up filming. Closer to seeing our film as a whole. And last but not least, closer to showing you all *The Wraith: Eyes of Judgment.*

Right now as I take a break from compiling footage from Friday's shoot, I thought I should go ahead and do another Lair Line and update everyone on what's going on. Friday we shot a crucial scene in the film. One of my personal favorites from the script as well. The scene: the Cobra visits Latham for a deal of a lifetime. We had to rush into getting this scene shot actually. The office was going to close down today actually, and we had limited time to pull Rick McVey and Ryan Basham together and prepare for this scene. With limited time, we were able to pull it off indeed, and pull it off beyond my expectations.

The scene went very well, and the two performances in this scene are nothing short of breathtaking. I wish I could go into detail about the content of the scene, but I can't. I can say that this is a pivotal moment in the film, and Rick and Ryan achieved greatness together. Hitchcock said that a film is only as good as its villain. Well, in this little baby we have two villains, and they are both superb and very evil. When I think of the characteristics of a villain, I think someone who has no soul, forgiveness, or heart. Someone who is evil to the bone and has no remorse for his or her actions. Rick and Ryan both bring this across in their roles. I'm not going to lie when I say you will be surprised at how the slightest body movement from either of these actors coveys how truly evil they are. Both guys did a phenomenal job and I can't wait to work with them again.

Last week, Assistant Director and Producer, Ty Kelsey and I went out and got some exterior shots. We had planned another pickup shot with David and Stacie Cooper, but snow and cold weather hindered those plans, which was the same as today. Apparently, we're in the middle of a winter storm. Take out the snow and the overall look to our city is perfect for shooting now. We're getting a lot of rain, too, which washes away the snow pretty fast and leaves a grayish look to everything. With the overcast sky, we're able to get awesome shots this time of year.

Today while I compiled footage for Alex Riback, the Editor, and more FX shots to send off to the FX Supervisor, I figured I'd update everyone really quick on what the next month holds. Next week, we're filming the whole opening sequence to the film. The Wraith Online's Forum member "Seven" is driving up next weekend to help us out. Expect some sort of news update or set report from him soon thereafter.

The week after that we'll probably just do some small pickup shots we need to get done. The third week in February, Scott Leva will be coming out to help us get the final fight scene shot. Expect a lot of cool stuff to surface after that shoot. After that, we'll resume filming in March and by the end of March, we should be done with the film. I've sent footage off to be worked on already, and I'll be sending even more out this week, while preparing for the shoot with Seven.

Also on the horizon is a second and full length trailer, a couple more web documentaries, and pictures galore. Everything is shaping up nicely on the film now, and we're heading into the home stretch. We're at about 80-85% complete on the shooting, so not much longer now. I'm really excited to get this film done. I need a break from filming and want to focus on the promotion for this film for starters, but more importantly, I can't wait to see this thing come to life and watch it from beginning to end. I have high expectations for this film, and once you all see it you'll understand why. I predict a pretty good sized buzz about this film once it's released. Remember, you heard that from here first.

Another Lair Line next weekend, so until then...

Stephen

<u>February 7 2005</u>

Well, well, well. The opening semi-action sequence to the film is shot and bagged. What a blast the past two days have been. Mucho thanks goes out to Seven for driving up SEVEN hours to have TWO whole lines in this film. This guy believed so much in this film from the beginning that we had to take care of him. And that's exactly what we did. Then we beat the complete and total crap out of him. Literally. Let me explain...

Wednesday, the guy originally playing the thug Otto in the opening sequence and I had an altercation and I basically told him where to go. I was desperate. I had backups but couldn't get a hold of them and prepare them in enough time. Seven was all ready to come up from Birmingham, everything was all planned with the rest of the cast and crew. Then this total jerk off decides he wants to sever ties with Sir Reel and I. Ok, no big deal, but I was concerned for a minute. Now, my good buddy and Sir Reel regular Dietrich Adetayo suggested his friend Joey Hale for the role of Otto. I had met Joey and knew him through Big D, but that was it. The only thing I really remember about him is that he said if I ever needed someone's ass kicked on camera, give him a call. I called him. Joey agreed, saw the script just 5 hours before shooting, got into character, and totally surprised us all with his understanding of acting and filmmaking. I was shocked and glad the original guy left because now I can't see Otto played by anyone else. He was fantastic. Thanks, Joey!

Now, Seven came in yesterday, and was early even. Earlier yesterday I booked him a hotel, in fact the same hotel we shot Cobra scenes in last year. Ah, memories....Anyway, Seven showed up at my house last night and was entertained from the start. First off, I showed him the costume and watched as his eyes lit up like a child at Christmas. Then I showed him a cut of "Home of Darkness" and various scenes and clips from the film. He was totally shocked and will tell you his own thoughts himself, so I won't go into anymore details there. We ate some pizza and talked about movies and basically got to know one another better. Turns out, he's a really cool guy and was glad he came up. I wish I could have given him a bigger part, but the one he had really took its toll on him physically. For those who don't know, he's a small guy and soft-spoken. Imagining him as a thug was hard at first, but he immediately started throwing ideas out to me and I could see him as the thug Mikey. A LOT of ideas he came up with will make it into the final film, so he should be proud we gave him the freedom to collaborate with us on his character development. Subtle nuances he came up with really brought a two-dimensional character into reality. Great job, man! Very proud of you!

Now, I picked him up at the motel about noon and from there we went downtown to the locations. We had an hour before Joey met up with us, and Ty Kelsey and Rob Nelson were running a little late. Ty is always late and will be late for his own wedding and funeral. I've come to realize to plan early with Ty so we can start on time. Love ya, man, but you're a tardy fool! Anyway, Rob was our light technician for the day, and after today, will be asked back quite frequently. He's more than a gaffer to me.

Before Seven got to meet Joey, Ty, and Rob; I took him around the corner to the local comic book shop where I dwell. It was literally a block in front of where we shot part of the sequence, we had time to kill, so we went in. Who was there you ask? None other than my man Dietrich playing Hero Clix against a ten-year-old. After about 5 minutes in the store, we left and met up with Ty and Rob. Then Joey showed about 10 minutes after that and we were off to rehearsals.

We rehearsed part of the sequence numerous times and these guys ran their butts off. Over and over, Joey and Seven kept doing this sequence and really pulling it together creatively based on the original shot synopsis I gave. They had good chemistry together, too, which made for easy adaptation in the alleys. They really gave rehearsals their all and

I was very happy going into the night shoot. Basically we started filming about 6:15 and had about 3-4 hours before David Cooper would even be on set. So we set out to get everything shot that we could before The Wraith showed himself.

When he came, he brought fellow partner in crime Randy Stout (8-Ball) with him. It was good to see Randy on set again. He was there mainly for moral support, but added his input as well and helped shape the action part of the sequence to what it is now. We basically followed the script verbatim in the shots we took, but improvised some of it to fit the actors and what they had previously shot. All in all, I'm very pleased and proud of the hard work that went into tonight's shoot. We shot basically the first three pages of the script and I can say that this is one opening to a comic book film nobody will see coming. It's impressive to say the least and the performances given were truly spectacular.

Now, some injuries did occur. While rehearsing one shot, Joey basically ran straight into a wall and jammed his toe up really good. After that, he kind of limped, but still gave 100 percent of everything he had to give. This took place before Cooper even made it to set, so we still had enough left to shoot to really take a toll on him. He let us know his foot was hurting but urged us he was OK and to continue on. Seven's character was pushed around by Joey repeatedly before even facing The Wraith. I could tell it was wearing him down, so we took a pizza break and then Cooper showed up. Once David got there, he proceeded to throw both of the thugs repeatedly into a metal garage door. He slammed them both around and really let them have it, BUT this is all the magic of filmmaking. Though these guys did their own stunts, they toughed it out and got through it and gave top-notch performances, even though they were bruised and beaten up. Seven took some really hard knocks into the door, so expect his stuff to look really sick onscreen.

Well, the shoot is done for this week. Next week we're taking off and the week after that Scott Leva should be in town to help us nail the final fight sequence. Each shoot keeps getting better and better, and this film is really taking a life of its own. I want to personally thank Ty, Rob, Randy, Cooper, and last but certainly not least, I want to thank Joey and Seven for their excellent performances and for the heart they put into these roles. I know they're just thugs, but these thugs have names and are portrayed with such realism that it's almost scary. I can't wait for everyone to see this stuff and just know it's not going to be much longer.

Until Next Time...

Stephen

February 13 2005

Sacrifice. It not only describes the story of the newest superhero film, *The Wraith: Eyes of Judgment*, but the story behind it as well. I met with the director, Stephen Semones, at his home, in Bristol, Tennessee, late the Friday before last. Stephen sacrifices a large portion of his paycheck to see that this film gets made, all the while having enough to pay the bills and put food on the table. We spent the first part of the night looking at The Wraith costume, eating very good pizza, and talking about comic book movies. Then it was time to get down to the business of the day that lay ahead.

Stephen showed me his work area, a cozy kind of office that shared room with his hall of fame (pictures and memorabilia of famous people). We then started looking at several pieces from the still unfinished film. We went through some very good scenes between Robert Latham, played by Rick McVey and Charlie Grieco, played by David Semones; scenes between The Wraith (David Cooper, who is referred to as Coop) and Leena Patterson (Stacie Cooper); as well as bloopers (very funny). However, for these pieces, it wasn't just the acting and script that stood out. It was the lighting and camera positions; it was the little things that were found by paying close attention to the film. Things that can separate a good film from a bad one, things that make movies spectacular. After the prep work was done, Stephen showed his generosity again by setting me up in a hotel room. During my time spent at his house, I also had the honor of meeting his wife and young son. At the age of four, his knowledge of superheroes could easily put many to shame.

As Stephen showed me around the next day, I realized why Bristol was the perfect location for filming. At first glance we see a city that tries to put on a bright and shiny face. A city that builds new, technologically innovative libraries, a city that is on the move, a city that reinvents itself. However, underneath that bright and shiny makeup is a city that is falling apart. You can't see it at first, the little empty buildings, the crumbling separating brick, the homeless, and the despair, but it slowly creeps into your system and soon it is the only thing that you see. This city (like the one in the *Eyes of Judgment*) needs saving.

After going around a bit, Stephen took me to the local comic book shop. This is where we met Dietrich Adetayo (the special effects coordinator). We then went to the locations that he was going to shoot later that night.

As we were going about from location to location, we finally met up with his assistant director (Tyrell Kelsey) and his assistant (who Stephen lovingly refers to as Bitch 1 and Bitch 2). As we continued our journey, I had the great time of talking to Tyrell. Tyrell, like Stephen, is making sacrifices for this film. His dedication to this project far succeeds that of his education. In order to make this film, he is taking a semester off of school. More on Tyrell later. After Tyrell and his assistant talked to me for a while we met up with Otto played by Joey Hale. Joey was not originally cast to play Otto, but was picked at the last minute after Stephen had some disagreements with the original actor.

Now it was time for the rehearsing/shooting, which we spent all day on. On this day, I looked past the script, the acting, and the special effects. I truly wish that this was the story that the audiences were going to see. This was not one man directing a movie, but a whole cast. They conversed, disagreed, and most importantly showed their passion for this film. A passion that puts even the greatest directors in Hollywood to shame. What if, I thought to myself, all movies could be filmed like this? If stupid egos and that damn money were put aside and then passion would be the only thing to guide a film. I say this especially of Tyrell. As I saw him spout out ideas (which some we took and others we didn't), show me the quaintness of sound as he ate potato chips in front of the camera (I had earphones on, listening on what sounds the camera's microphone picked up), and direct several scenes I noticed a glimmer of genius. A glimmer of genius I hope is recognized one day.

It was during rehearsal/shooting where Joey made his sacrifice. Even though he wasn't originally cast, Joey made a point of making his character stand out. For Stephen, perhaps it was this opening scene that his whole film was to ride on, if this first scene fails it may prove disaster for the whole film. In order to make this character, The Wraith, believable (the whole movie counted on the believability of a "ghost like" superhero scaring the crap out of criminals and their mob bosses) the reaction of these first characters that The Wraith meets has to be believable. Realizing this, Joey gained cuts, scrapes, bruises, and a busted toe (he accidentally ran into a wall and had to limp throughout the rest of the shoot).

After the main scenes were shot, it was almost time for The Wraith to show up. For me, I couldn't wait, after seeing footage of how well the costume turned out...I just had to see this for myself. The Wraith showed up around eight or nine in the evening (with his friend Randy Stout—who plays Eight Ball in the film). I couldn't have met a more down to earth actor in my life. David Cooper has the rare talent of turning his Wraith character on and off at will. While the camera was rolling David Cooper was The Wraith and while they were off, he entertained us with several Rodney Dangerfield jokes. He had made his own sacrifices as well, but what they were, he would never tell. With him, the cast and crew began filming their final scenes. As the final scenes were being shot the cast and crew had to deal with the cold weather, their weary bodies, farts, and sexual advances from The Wraith himself (whether they were wanted or unwanted remains to be seen...lol).

There I was, after all of the handshakes and "thank yous", in my hotel room thinking on the whole day. I began my set report as things still remained fresh in my memory. And now it has come down to the sad facts. Now it has come down to the harsh reality. It would be a nice world where hard workers could get their way; however, it is not that kind of world. One question lingered in my mind—Is this film going to be successful? By that I mean financially successful. There is a great chance that it won't. The odds are stacked against it, heavily. Or are they? Stephen Semones is planning to show this film at conventions in England and here in the States (*and getting a cinema release* - Frank). Even Hollywood is going to have a look at his latest invention. *Hellboy* and *Blade II* director, Guillermo del Toro, is going to receive a copy of this film. Once again, for those of you who skipped the line above, Guillermo del Toro IS going to see this film. That fact alone is enough to get some people excited. However, Stephen can't think of that right now. I mentioned to him that this film could explode into something much bigger. He admits when he looks at this little project he doesn't think of that possibility. Well, he better start. So perhaps a better question is this: will all of these sacrifices be for naught? Perhaps that is the easiest question to answer.

I would like to thank Stephen for asking to me to come up to visit with him as he filmed his movie, a movie that has taken more than just time out of this young director. *The Wraith: Eyes of Judgment* comes out in June, 2005. I, for one, wish it all the best.

Adam Oravec aka Mikey aka Seven

March 1 2005

Well, right now I'm watching the Oscars and I'm suffering the second hour blahs. Anyway, this sparks some thought in me as I sit and watch this brainless brown-nosing. Anyhow, apparently there are short film achievements at the Academy Awards. This brings me to thinking back over the course of filming *The Wraith*, and though not Oscar-worthy, we have achieved more than we ever set out to and will be delivering a tremendous film.

This brings me to thinking—will we win any awards for the film? Will it bring a cult following? Will people love/hate it? I don't have the answers to these questions, but what I can tell you from having this week off from my real job to play "catch up" and get more of this film done, we're going to break the boundaries of no-budget filmmaking. Is this deserving of an Academy Award? Honestly? Yes, it is. I plan on breaking boundaries with this film. There shouldn't be a line drawn by Hollywood in the sand. I believe I'm put here to help filmmakers prove that creativity will prevail over the system. Well, maybe not, but it's gonna be a fun battle.

I started my "vacation" on Monday and immediately started planning the next two months out. Though it's now Sunday and I still don't have all the holes filled, I know exactly what I have left to shoot and how I want to shoot. This week I spent two 12-hour days back to back in front of my camera and computer. I went through 15 tapes (that's 15 hours) worth of footage and compiled it down to two and a half tapes for Alex the editor and about half a tape for Marc, the FX guru. I went through every shot and copied each take I thought we could use. This is VERY, VERY time consuming and can lead to goggle eyes, cramped eyebrows, and wrist crackling. I suffered through it and in about 3 or 4 days, these guys are going to have everything we've shot thus far. I've seen some stuff already from Marc and Alex I must say, everyone is going to be SHOCKED!!!

Yesterday we were scheduled to shoot on top of an 8-story building. The maintenance man whom I spoke to twice this week assured me he'd show up to let us in so we'd have access to the roof. Guess what?? He never showed. I called him 1 hour after he was supposed to show up and basically he had no excuse other than laziness. This screwed up my shot, but as always, I had a contingency plan. I took external shots of the building in hopes that our FX wizard, Marc, can use it somehow for what we had planned.

We were shooting two scenes and two different "shots" for the film. One scene was scheduled for on top of the building, which I had to change to alley-level, and I was honestly pissed at this point. I had David Cooper in costume. It was literally about 30 degrees at 10 pm and I had my four year old son Sean with me visiting the shoot. A building and its warmth were far from us at this point. The last shoot we were on we were asked to leave the alley. We had a backup anyway, but still. It's the trials of no-budget filmmaking. Now, what I did shoot was wonderful.

I had done the voice-overs for these scenes on Thursday with Nathan Blevins (Max), so I shaped our changed location scene around the dialogue Nathan done. It worked perfectly and will blend very well into the next part once edited. My only real gripe is the lack of rooftop scenery, but the new location is very creepy and gothic in appearance and will blend smoothly into the next scene.

The last scene we shot was another voice-over scene that I did part of with Nathan on Thursday as well. It's basically of The Wraith prowling the streets and alleys and receives a call from Max. This scene will take place near the end of the film (hint, hint) and the angle is just perfect to blend with the music and impending climax. It's a scene that will be one single shot/angle and will look VERY cool when edited together.

We basically have five shoots left and we're done. This could be like five or six weeks, but we're almost there. Tomorrow I'm mailing off everything we've shot thus far so post-production will be short once we wrap. I'll be sending more footage as we go and hopefully by June or July, all our questions will be answered. The Wraith is coming very soon and I assure everyone that this will surprise you. Reviewing everything we've done so far in shooting this week has opened my eyes to what all the hard work has gone to. I'm proud to have been a part of this filmmaking endeavor and I'm proud of everyone involved. It's been a tough road, but worth every step of the way so far. Thanks to everyone involved and who has worked so hard in making this fanboy's dream come true. I can't wait to see you all on the "red carpet"...ha!

Until Next Time...

Stephen

<u>March 22 2005</u>

I'm not ready for this. That's exactly what I said Tuesday morning. I spent Monday night reviewing the script and making my little infamous storyboards. I was about to (over the course of two nights) film what was the emotional explosion in the film. Taking place at the climax, our beloved Michael Reeve and Leena Patterson come to a cross-road in their relationship. Was I ready to film this? No. Did I have to? Yes. My problem isn't because of lack of faith in the script/actors/crew etc. It was because this is the first time filming something so emotionally deep as these 6.5 pages from the script. I feel somewhat uncomfortable trying to (as the director) pull such emotions from my cast. I'm used to comedic dialogue, or shooting people, etc., and this was a complete opposite shoot from what I'm used to.

We were only able to shoot basically after 8pm on Tuesday and Thursday night. If we didn't get done Thursday, we'd carry it over to Saturday and wrap then. Luckily, we got it in two days. The cast called for David and Stacie Cooper and Nathan Blevins. Nathan comes and goes throughout these 6.5 pages, so naturally we broke it up. Nathan could only be there Thursday night, so Tuesday we shot as much as possible without him.

The scene originally called for the location to be in a bedroom. Well, late last week I decided we really couldn't get a bedroom that would suit us all without shooting on a greenscreen. I've already gave Marc Kimball (the FX Wizard!—He's like Gandalf—makes magic happen!) enough greenscreen headache, so the probable solution was to change the location. I thought about it and realized my parents were going out of town. They have a nice living room that could work...so...hey, Mom? Can I use your house?

Needless to say, when the Coopers arrived Tuesday night at my parents house, they were also nervous about what we were about to film. It's because we're all used to a different style of filmmaking. These two nights of filming were about to whip our asses and we knew it. Ty was with me both nights easing my burden. He kept assuring me that we had nothing to worry about and I kept assuring him I had my concerns. I can write emotional, but can I direct it? That was it. That was what I kept thinking about. Then we started. After a few rough takes, we got through the first two shots with ease. Then we started rolling with the environment, each other, and the script.

We created greatness out of fear.

Stephen

March 24 2005

Feeling much better about the upcoming night shoot, I decided to take it easy and capture Tuesday's footage for Alex Riback (editor). Anyway, as I captured, I noticed something. We are making a REALLY GOOD movie here. Playing it back I could see how much the cast were enjoying their roles. I could see it in their eyes. Though they're not professional actors, they were enjoying the freedom of the roles and it shows through.

We got to the location, but this time with Nathan. We had to wait a bit on the Coopers to arrive, but once they did, it was the same tension again. Can we pull this off again? Between my wonderful comments of the previous shoot, and Nathan there to fulfill his acting and dialogue coaching duties, it wasn't long before we were off filming and half-way done. We flew through it with a vengeance. After the initial few rough takes at the beginning of the night, it was nailed take after take after take to a golden perfection. It got to the point where all of us were throwing out ideas for the shots/scenes/dialogue inflections/etc., and we were all enjoying it. The fear of bringing these emotions out scared us all. We were scared of the result we could get. Looking back, I'm glad I was scared. I'm glad David and Stacie were scared. It allowed us to step outside the box and deliver a non-traditional look at a love story. It also allowed us to explore ourselves and collaborate as a group.

We went through group therapy in two nights, but at 1:30 Friday morning, I called "wrap." That was it. Before we knew it, we were done. Great footage, awesome performances, and we achieved what we thought we may not be able to do. We're all proud now of what it took from us to do these 6.5 pages of script.

Thursday night was also kind of a sad time for us all. We're now finished with everything Nathan and Stacie are in, so they're no longer required for filming. They're done and just going to sit back and wait for the premiere. Well, Nathan won't because he'll be there coaching dialogue and throwing out his patented "Nathanisms." I'd like to take a minute and say that it was my pleasure filming these two actors and I can't wait to show them all their hard work.

That goes to show you how close we are to wrapping this thing up. We are literally this close to finishing this baby up and releasing it upon the world. I'll be releasing another webdoc really soon. I know about every Lair Line I say that, but I've got one in progress now and hope to have it finished within a week.

I hope everyone is looking close to seeing this film. We'll be sending out a press release for the premiere at the Abingdon Cinemall, so be sure to mark your calendars.

Until Then...

Stephen

April 11 2005

Fate. I believe in it...but not as in all the time. I believe you know when fate happens and recognize it as fate. Fate is destiny being dropped right in your lap and you dealing with it the best way you can. Be it in acknowledging that it is fate and making the best of it, or going about your daily business and thinking that everything happens just because.

About two weeks ago, some guy emailed me about working with me. I get emails like this all the time. Do you need this, do you need that, can I help with this, whatcha think of that? This is basically what they all say. This one was really no different, except that the guy contacting me this time lived really close to me. Around a thirty-minute drive up the interstate. His name is Trevor Carter. Trevor contacted me telling me he was a musician, but was also interested in making a film in other aspects. Now, I replied as I always do appreciating the offer, but I didn't need a musician. I need other things, so I said since he lived so close by, he was more than welcome to come down today for the shoot.

Tonight we did pick up shots from a scene we shot back in September. Seven months back we did a scene with Mandi Leigh and recently decided that we wanted a couple of close-ups we just overlooked back then. Nothing major, but we also wanted to test out our new Steadi-cam, so this was a good opportunity to bring in someone new. We weren't doing anything really exciting, but by God we made it fun. We had to wait until it got dark to shoot, so that left us there for around a half hour just talking and having a blast.

Around seven tonight Ty Kelsey showed up with Zek Hensley at my house for the shoot. Shortly thereafter, Randy Stout showed. Randy had to play make-up artist and draw the tattoos on Zek for the scene. Being a professional tattoo artist (he didn't need his drawn on for the shoot), he was able to turn Zek into Chainz within a few minutes. Trevor called me letting me know he was in town early, so realizing it was going to be a good shoot, we headed out the door. Once we got downtown five minutes later, we met Trevor and headed a few blocks over to the location.

Now, this is where I get technical about stuff. We had to do close-ups and filler shots with the thugs Eight Ball (Randy) and Chainz (Zek), but we had to do this seven months later and do it without Mandi. Basically, when we did close-ups, Nathan Blevins or Ty would fill in for Mandi so the other two could have a visual reference. Though they weren't near as attractive as Mandi, they served their purpose. I had to make sure that we got the shot we needed and do it so that the audience won't even know that Mandi wasn't standing there. Even though we did close-ups, we did a few angles that weren't too close and we had to position the camera just right to make sure that the place where Mandi was supposed to be wasn't shown. We had to judge and get the perspectives just right to make this work. When doing something seven months later, this isn't easy to recreate. Heck, this isn't easy to do period, but we got this done and I am VERY pleased with the end results.

Zek and Randy did great again, and we found a great cameraman in Trevor. He impressed us all and we realize that fate directed him to us. I understand why he was brought to us, and I hope he understands why himself. People like him don't just fall out of the sky and start working on movies, but Trevor just appeared from nowhere ready and willing. He did a good job and letting him run the camera freed me up to do my part as director. I feel that pushing me back to watch helped me gain a better view of things and I can see the scene better from standing back than on a three-inch monitor. We all just wish Trevor could have gotten in on this thing from the start, but there's always the next film.

I'd like to let everyone know that we're almost done shooting. We wanted to be done sooner, but I want you all to know that the wait will pay off. We apologize for the delay, but realize we've been working on this film since August of 2003, and we're now in the home stretch. We're winding down and after next weeks shoot, we'll only have three shoots left. A lot of the FX work is done and I can't tell everyone often enough how much this film is going to shock and surprise. From the opening to the very end, this is going to be one hell of a ride! I hope you all enjoy it because it's been a blast making this film.

Until Next Time...

Stephen

<u>April 18 2005</u>

What can I say? We have three shoots left on the film and I'm getting really excited. Today we traveled to our new warehouse for a critical scene in the film.

After waiting for Ty to arrive (as usual), Trevor, David Cooper, Ty, and myself all headed about 30 minutes away for the shoot about 10:30 this morning. My brother David was supposed to meet us there, and when we got there, he was waiting for us. As impatient as he is, I guess he didn't mind the wait. Why would he? I mean, he was only shooting a MAJOR segment of the film today and probably the defining moment of his character, Charlie Grieco. Rick McVey was supposed to meet up with us after lunch, so we had to get as much shot as we could before he got there. David Cooper had to be somewhere early afternoon and Rick had a play in the evening. Needless to say, we couldn't waste any time.

Now, I don't want to say what scene we shot because it will spoil all the fun, but just imagine The Wraith, Charlie Grieco, Robert Latham, and a couple of thugs in a warehouse. Like I said, this was a CRUCIAL segment of the film, so we had to take our time, but get it all shot in the small timeframe we had. We pulled through on the time aspect, but we got off to a slow start. Nathan Blevins showed up to assist behind the scenes and add his input.

For some reason, we couldn't get the opening shot timed right. The Wraith would walk too far, the thugs would come in too late, Grieco missed his mark...you get the point. We must have spent 15 takes on the first shot before we got a good one. However, once we got it nailed, it was really cool! Really, really cool!! We did everything we could before Rick got there, and had just finished cleaning up some "blood" when he arrived. Once he got there, he changed into Latham, stepped onto the set, walked through it twice and was ready to roll. I set the last shot up of the scene. We basically only needed Rick for about fifteen seconds on film. Literally. He's only in two shots, but those two shots are absolutely amazing. About twenty minutes later we were done. Rick's part was so small in this, I almost hated getting him down for it. He was really cool about it and understood that we needed him to make this scene. It didn't take long once the cameras rolled on Rick to wrap up for the day.

When I got home, I immediately began cutting this segment of the film. I just now finished a rough cut and I'm about to email it to Frank. Today was a really productive day for us here at Sir Reel and things are really moving into high gear on the post-production end. Trevor and I have already started cutting the fight scene that Mandi Leigh was a part of. We've got it about 70% complete and should have it cut really soon. It's getting closer...are you all ready??

Stephen

<u>May 13 2005</u>

Well, what can I say? Post production. Man, it's tough. It's literally like writing the film all over again. I compare it to a putting a puzzle together. I've got all these pieces: the script, the music, the footage, the voice overs, etc., and I have to put it together in a coherent format that moves along at a good pace.

Right now, I have a rough cut of the film. It's about 35 minutes long and is missing a couple of shots here and there, but I'm almost there. We've got about 10 more minutes of footage to shoot and edit in and we're done. Right now Marc Kimball is finishing up his second batch of FX work and is awaiting the footage we shoot for some minor work. Voodoo Studios have already began the sound design and Foley FX for the film and are receiving a shipment of video and audio this week. Jonathan at Voodoo told me that it will take around two months for the Foley, sound design, and digital mix. They've already begun the initial steps, so we're looking at having their final master in July. Marc Kimball's work is almost complete as well, so I can safely say that things are winding down.

What has been going on is that due to editing issues, I have had to tackle this project myself. Well, at first I thought I would be editing by myself, but Trevor Carter came on board, so I've got a partner in crime now to tackle this with me. Trevor has been a tremendous help in helping me edit this film. Several scenes you will see in the final cut, Trevor edited himself and without me even being present. One of the scenes he cut is an awesome scene between Robert Latham and the Cobra. He's been a valuable asset since his arrival and my only regret is that he wasn't with us from the start of this film. We've got him now though and we're glad!

Like I said, we've got about 35 minutes of the film cut, so I can go ahead and tell you how it's shaping up. This isn't your typical comic book film. Yes, it's based on a comic book character, but it's more than that. It's not off the wall like *Spider-Man*, and *The Wraith* isn't conflicted like *Batman*. Therefore, he's not your run of the mill superhero. I love the others I just mentioned, but you cannot compare this film to those. To me, this film seems a lot more intimate and personal than others I've seen. Its small scale makes it seem very realistic and original. As far as the pacing, well it opens with a burst of action, so you take that however you need. After the opening, the film immediately begins to tell the parallel origin of The Wraith and the Cobra.

In Act Two we see the impact that the origins have from Act One on Leena Patterson, Robert Latham, and Charlie Grieco. In Act Three, the storylines all come down to one final moment—Judgment. You may ask, "Stephen, can you be any more cryptic?" Yes I can. However, I will spoil this no further. This film is very emotionally driven. Each character has their own emotion and mood, so that is what really propels the story at a nice pace. The editing really takes a backseat to the story when it all boils down to it. Everything comes second place to the story when you think about it.

Well, I'm hoping to deliver to you all an exciting, intriguing, and beautiful story that you will hopefully watch over and over for years to come. As far as I can tell, we're making history here. Everyone who has seen any cuts of the film has been nothing short of impressed and wanting to see more, so expect something truly special this August.

Yes, I said August.

Until Next Time...

Stephen

June 8 2005

We would now like to formally announce the release date for *The Wraith: Eyes of Judgment* at the Abingdon Cinemall in Abingdon, Virginia, USA. The date is set—19 August 2005! Mark that down in your calendars, and if you live in the area or are able to travel there for the premiere, please let us know by visiting the Attend the Premiere section of the website. We hope to see you there.

Frank

June 17 2005

We're done filming. The movie is completely shot. I've been working feverishly the last two weeks to finalize everything we had left to shoot and edit. I mailed the film off to Voodoo Studios, Adam DiTroia, and Marc Kimball for them to add their finishing touches. While they work their magic I'll be tweaking the film (possibly some minor pickup shots) and getting the DVD ready for the September release. We also have a final date set for the premiere at the Cinemall—August 19th. That day also happens to be my birthday (*and my mother's* - Frank), which ironically worked out that way without my influence or control.

The last month of filming had its ups and downs off screen. I won't go into detail on that but we all pulled together and finished shooting the movie. I've literally spent the last two weeks glued to my computer editing the film as well, but that's another story all together. The last things we had to shoot were the final fight scene and the BIG dialogue sequence before it involving the three main villains. My hat goes off to everyone involved shooting these last two scenes. They really poured their blood, sweat, and tears into the last stretch to ensure we got the best ending to the film that we could. Rick McVey, Ryan Basham, David Cooper, and David Semones acted their hearts out for the final segments of the film.

For the final fight, everything literally went smooth. I could go into all the details of each shot, but everyone will have a chance to see the film in two months anyway, so I'll just give out some other kind of "inside" information: injuries. There were basically very minor injuries during the final fight scene, however they were all inflicted by The Wraith himself. Chris Wolfe (Latham's Bodyguard) banged his toe up pretty good during a jump. Dietrich Adetayo (another bodyguard) got his mouth busted by a big Wraith head butt. My brother David, Charlie Grieco, literally took the most punishment. He actually got pistol whipped by The Wraith and his head busted open a small amount. Each of them that were hurt laughed it off (surprisingly) and did another take. There were minimal amounts of real blood, but I had to mention their efforts. They each bled to bring you all *The Wraith*. Though each incident was completely supervised, things happen, though this time it was minimal and didn't delay filming at all. These guys deserve the standing ovation when it's all said and done. Actually, the whole cast deserves one.

The minor injuries were nothing compared to the lengthy task I had trying to get this film completely pieced together. To put it simply, I had the whole film edited except for these last two scenes and two small pickup shots. As we ran close to the deadline, I was basically filming and editing at the same time. This got to be very stressful, but I pulled through. I'm really anxious to show this film to everyone and I can't wait for August. This is the last Lair Line that will deal with the filming aspect of the film. The next Lair Line will be really, really special I promise, but I'll finish up this one first. :) Expect another one really soon though.

If I had to sum up my experience shooting this film I guess I'd say the following: I gave two years of my life trying to make the best film I could. I've worked with so many talented people in person and via email (which is tough). I cannot thank each person enough for their individual contribution. I cannot even begin to express my gratitude to these men and women who have worked so hard to bring Frank's vision to life onscreen. I guess I've been the mediator in the whole collaboration and I'm nothing short of honored to have played my part. I guess Frank deserves his share of thanks. Most of all for giving a poor filmmaker like myself the opportunity to bring such an incredible world to life as a film. He's been with me (overseas) the whole journey and I thank him dearly. Making this film has not been easy. In fact, it's the hardest thing I've ever had to do. I really feel like Sir Reel Films has truly accomplished something. Regardless of its success, we all made a film that we had a blast making and can't wait to return to do a feature film version. Wrapping up filming was bittersweet, but I will miss it. We have 28 hours of footage and over 4,000 still pictures just for one 47 minute film. That's a lot to go back through for the stroll down memory lane, but I will always look back on this film as my first great achievement.

I sit on the eve of the Adventure Con, nervous and filled with anxiety. In fact, I just about had a panic attack. I know we'll do fine, but I can't be too at ease. I type this just before I head to bed and wake up and start our next journey. A journey this film has allowed us to take. We will be guests along side some legends (Robert Englund, Adam West) promoting this film and can't wait for their reaction. For now however, I should get my rest. Making this film has been a blast and I've loved it every step of the way. This is an amazing film and I hope you all enjoy it as much as we did making it. Well, off to the Adventure Con.

Peace!

Stephen

June 21 2005

FRIDAY June 17 - I woke up after about 4 hours of nervous sleep. I realized something the night before that I hadn't thought of before—We're about to attend our first convention and are we ready (and worthy) to be there. We were soon about to see.

My wife, son, and I took off to Knoxville around 10am. The car ride down was a nervous one for me. I was anxious to find out how people would take us and if we'd be taken serious at all. Little did I know I was in for the best weekend of my entire life.

We didn't do much on Friday. We got to the convention center and picked up our passes, checked out our table, and basically left. We had to get a few things and decided to come early Saturday and set up. Our table area wasn't that big so it wouldn't take long to set up. The family and I decided to spend some time together before catching up with a friend we were staying with. We drove all over Knoxville and had a blast before traveling to my friend Brian's house for the evening. I went to bed more nervous than ever.

SATURDAY July 18 - Ryan Basham had come in with his friend Friday night and had given us all the info on his hotel and such. I awoke Saturday morning realizing that my brother David wouldn't be there until about 11 and it started at 9:30. I was curious to see how he reacted to the crowd I saw gathering as I made it to the Convention Center.

As I got to my tables I realized who was around me. Directly behind me was Captain Marvel himself, Jackson Bostwick. He was a really nice guy and chatted with us all weekend. He came by the table and checked out *The Wraith* trailer. He liked what he saw and thus he was presented with a free comic.

As the day progressed Ryan Basham and I were really promoting our table to everyone who passed. We had on display two large movie posters behind us and three spread out on our tables which were surrounded by comics. To the side we had running a trailer and an FX Documentary. We took 40 comics with us and in two days came back with 1, so all in all it was a good trip. We gave, like, 4 away. Jackson Bostwick, Adam West, and John Rhys-Davies were but three that received a complementary issue of The Wraith # 0. The day was going great and I couldn't believe the response to the trailer and comic. We had a signup sheet for a Premiere and DVD mailer and got a couple of pages full of people who want to attend the premiere or buy the DVD.

When I met John Rhys-Davies, it was in the afternoon. Things had calmed down; the lines had died, so we were able to approach him. My brother, Ryan, and I walked straight up to him and started up a conversation about who we were. He was such a pleasant man and a gentleman. We invited him to our booth to check out our trailer. He (to our complete surprise) stood up and told his assistants that he'd be back. He then walked with us (unsupervised) across the floor to our table. He stopped occasionally to grab a camera and snap a picture of himself, or to shake someone's hand, but he was on a mission with us to see *The Wraith* trailer. When we all arrived at the table my wife and friend Brian were completely shocked to see our new friend. He introduced himself to everyone and casually checked out our booth. He took a comic and started looking at the trailer. He liked what he saw and told us "good job!" He was impressed with our efforts as filmmakers. He stood there with us for about 10 minutes and just gave out advice. The things he said to us I won't repeat, but those who were there truly got words of wisdom from a legend. After chatting with us, he posed for a picture with us and then one with my son. After leaving our table he stood around the center floor and just talked to fans and hung out. He is truly a class act and an extremely nice and approachable man. Thank you, Mr. Davies. Thank you for everything you said and your advice. We hope you love the comic. ;)

After that success we felt nothing could top it. Then I ran into an old friend who is now a film journalist. William Wright walked straight up to the booth and for the first time in 9 years, we spoke face to face. What a great feeling it was catching up with him. He then told me that when the convention ended for the day at 7, he had an interview with Robert Englund. I talked him into letting me meet Mr. Englund. He agreed and we spent the rest of the day there catching up and hanging out. My wife and son left to go back home with my mom, so we had nothing to do but network and socialize. Come 7pm, the only two celebrity guests left were Robert Englund and John Davies. We packed up, met up with William, and headed over to the celeb tables. There were only about 10 people left hanging around for last minute autographs, but these two men stayed until everyone was satisfied and had their chance.

We walked up to Mr. Davies and thanked him for his time at our booth. He then began to talk to us for another 15 minutes as Mr. Englund finished up. He was very polite and energetic about us being filmmakers and going after this ourselves. He said goodbye to us and left. We stood there with one man left—Robert Englund. As he finished up, William approached him and Robert invited him out to dinner. William asked if I could come and they agreed. They took a car and I walked a couple blocks away to a really nice restaurant. The rest of Sir Reel Films unloaded our stuff and then came to the restaurant. When I walked in I saw William and Robert and Nancy Englund sitting at the bar. I was greeted by them and they told me to sit down. I took a seat beside his wife Nancy and talked to her as William interviewed Robert. Nancy Englund was a sweet and kind lady and I can't thank her enough for a wonderful and delightful conversation. We talked a little business but kept everything social and fun. As Robert was being interviewed, some of the workers at the bar asked for an autograph. He stopped the interview, grabbed some photos then started signing away. He was such a nice and generous man to everyone in his presence. I honestly feel that he's never met a stranger.

As our table was ready, we went outside. I sat with Robert, Nancy, William, Stephen (Robert's Agent), and a guy (name escapes me) from the Adventure Con. At the table beside us, the rest of Sir Reel Films sat as my support group. I couldn't believe I was having dinner with Freddy Krueger. I grew up watching this man and was terrified of him. Now I'm having dinner with him and his wife and he's one of the nicest men I've ever met. We sat there for about three hours as William interviewed him off and on. Informal and formal. I'm not sure how his interview will play out when he's done, but I can't wait to read it. After the interview we all talked about life, movies, music, love, and a lot more. When it was time for Robert and company to leave, he paid for everything. I mean everything. To top my night off, Robert Englund bought my dinner. I honestly felt as if I was about to die. He was so cool to us all. He talked to us as if we were his close friends and treated us the same.

After he left I was about to explode with excitement. A lot of things I can't repeat or go into detail on discussions or conversations, but Mr. Englund was full of advice and I was taken to school. Not just about films, but this charismatic man taught us all a little about ourselves and life in general. To him, his wife Nancy, and his agent, I say thank you for one of the best nights of my life. I'm still in complete shock it all happened the next day. When we left the restaurant, Sir Reel Films cut loose on the town of Knoxville. Once again, I can't give details, but fun was had by all!

SUNDAY July 19 - Waking up I had to confirm with others that the previous night had happened. Once they assured me that I had the night of my life, I snapped into reality (like 30 minutes later) and got ready to go to the convention center.

My brother, my friend Brian, and I arrived before Ryan. I got separated from my two partners in crime and found myself outside. Who materializes out of thin air and approaches me from behind? None other than John Davies. He literally startled me. We chatted briefly and then we parted ways. Needless to say, he remembered me. As I headed back downstairs to the convention room, I caught Davies walking through the early birds in line waiting for entrance and just talking to people. He was just hanging out. He loved it and was having a great time. This guy has no ego and is a true gentleman. He tried to stay for a second day, but he couldn't get his flight changed in time and had to leave. While he waited on his flight he hung out with everyone and eventually left just before the doors opened.

The crowd didn't pick up until after lunch, but seeing as it was Father's Day, it was to be expected. We hung out with some local authors, musicians, toy dealers, etc. We also got to talk a lot more to Jackson Bostwick and get to know him a little better. Come to find out, Captain Marvel lives pretty close to me. :) As the day ended and everyone said goodbye to the 2005 Knoxville Adventure Con, parting was bittersweet. I looked around and shopped for the first time just before we left. Last year I was there as a fan, this year I was there signing autographs and talking to a lot of interesting people.

I'd like to say thank you to everyone who stopped by and talked to us all. We hope you like your comics and look forward to seeing you all at the premiere. We hope you all check out the DVD as well. I'd also like to thank Ryan Basham, David Semones, and Brian Tittle for working the tables with me all weekend. These guys pulled their weight and really helped get this movie out to people. The reception from everyone was extremely positive, especially the established celebrities. I'd also like to thank Jackson Bostwick for a lovely time conversing with us. Hope to talk again with him soon. I'd like to thank John Rhys-Davies for disrupting the Adventure Con by being sociable and coming to our booth and hanging out with us. Thank you sir for your wisdom, enthusiasm, knowledge, and most of all, thank you for being an extremely nice guy! Last but certainly not least, thank you Nancy and Robert Englund. Thank you for dinner and the wonderful time I had. It was an honor and privilege to sit and toast margaritas with a legend. Thank you all.

Right now it's early Monday morning and I had to get this out while it was all fresh on my mind. Believe it or not, that mini-novel I just wrote is the condensed story. I'll send Frank some pictures and hopefully we'll be able to post them for everyone to see. I met a lot of great people and had a blast.

Until we all meet again...

Thanks for the memories.

Stephen

July 20th, 2005

Wow, almost two full years later and here I sit. Less than a few days of making two full years since I first agreed to do this film. Here I sit, a changed man. A changed filmmaker. I'm a better person now having done this film. My son had just turned three about the time I first decided to do this film. He turns five in five days. He was the main reason I decided to do this film. Growing up, I always dreamed of making a comic book movie and now I have. Though my perceptions have changed on everything from life down to comics, the magic is there for me to give my son. However, the great thing is, he's got to see me work the magic. He knows the cast and crew fairly well, and has spent hours beside me as I edited the film. He knows more about how movies are made than I'd say 90% of adults. This is my gift to him. *The Wraith: Eyes of Judgment*, it's all for him. For Sean. All my drive, inspiration, and creativity was put forth for him. Now that the film is complete, he now gets to see it at the theater and see his dad's gift to him enjoyed by a packed house. Now you all know why I was able to complete this film on a personal level. Now let me tell you how I was able to do it on a creative level.

When I first set out to make this film, I had a vision of what it would be. We have surpassed my original vision and I'm actually surprised at what we've achieved. I'll be getting the final print of the film this week. The sound is still being mixed and the score wrapped up, but we're almost there. I'll have the complete film, final sound and master print, around the first week or so of August ready to premiere at the Cinemall August 19th.

I want to personally thank everyone for their involvement, so bear with me. Let me start with the cast.

David Cooper - You know how much I love you, man, so I'm not even going to rattle a bunch of crap off. Thank you for wearing the Wraith suit and putting out one great performance in this role. You did wonderful, brother! Great job!

Ryan Basham - Your acting is only surpassed by your wit and charm. You are a great actor, but also a great friend. We've come a long way together in the short 2 plus years we've known one another, but I see a great future for us. Thanks for everything, including suffering the contact lens and makeup, but most of all...for suffering my horrible jokes. Have a margarita on me, Mr. Cobra.

Rick McVey - Rick, you are one talented man. Your presence as Robert Latham is intimidating and commanding. You were an asset to this film and your character takes us on one intense moment after another. As great as an actor that you may be, you are truly a class act and a great guy to have on set. I truly wish we could have had more time to work together, but I promise we'll work together again.

David Semones - What can I say? This is my brother, but he's also The Grieco. Charlie Grieco. I remember watching my brother progress as an actor over the course of this film. At the start of filming with him, he was paired with Rick McVey and was intimidated by his acting ability in comparison. David, from day one on *The Wraith* you impressed me as an actor. You have a natural ability to deliver dialogue and you play so well off the other actors. I truly feel there will be a David Semones fan club emerging from Charlie Grieco. I love you man, and glad I could help you meet John Davies.

Nathan Blevins - Our Max. Nathan studied his butt off to nail the Irish accent needed to play Max. Though about 15 to 18 years younger than the comic version of Max, Nathan pulled off a slight aging makeup effect along with the accent and brought Max to life. You did a great job Nathan! You're a talented actor and have such charisma on and offscreen.

Stacie Cooper - Almost last, but certainly not least. Your first acting job and you get the part of the girlfriend, Leena. A part that carries so much emotion, you gave 100%. Having to act with your husband has to be hard, especially being married to David. Thank you for doing this role and putting up with us all onset. I know we had a tough time, but we got through it and I'm proud of the hard work you put into Leena. Thank you.

As for the rest of the cast - Randy Stout, Mandi Leigh, Zek Hensley, Joey Hale, Adam Oravec, Dietrich Adetayo, Trevor Carter, Chris Wolfe, Izzy Real and that bum we paid a slice of pizza to do that one scene with Cooper—Thank you all. You all did great bringing Metro City to life. Thank you all for your hard work.

As for the technical crew of the film - Marc Kimball. You sir are a wizard. The Gandalf of special FX. Thank you for all your knowledge, support, and most of all, for all the man hours put into this movie. You're a one-man special FX team.

Xtreme Design FX & Universal Designs - Your creations helped us bring this character to the screen and helped us achieve the level of believability that we needed. Thank you all for the hard work and dedication to the vision we had. Great job!

Voodoo Studios - Jonathan and Dave. My hatchet men. My audio wave, hi-fi brothers of destruction. Without you guys, this film would only semi-rock. Now it rocks full swing and even hurts you if you turn it up too loud. You guys rule and you know I love your work and creativity. Thanks fellas for the hard work. Please, Dave, don't kill me just yet. We've got another movie coming up for me to make this up to you.

Adam DiTroia- My man from the north. My musically gifted brother. I wish we could have had more time to go back and forth on the score, but I love your work and you're a great friend. Thanks for taking my film to the next level and totally "getting it" and my twisted vision of how everything should fall into place.

Larry Groupe' - Thanks for "The Wraith Theme." It's truly a beautiful and epic theme and kicks off the film with a BANG. Your score totally encompasses the essence of the character and fits so well with the film. Thank you for your support and most of all, thank you for doing this film.

Trevor Carter - My right hand of doom. Trevor, you are my chief film chopper and I have nothing but respect for your slicing skills. Thanks for coming onboard and taking those cuts to the next level. Great cameraman, editor, musician, and stunt man. You got it all going for ya, brother!

For the rest of the crew and producers and everyone else involved—Derik Nutter, Ty Kelsey, Zek Hensley, Scott Leva, Jonathan Long, Christie Turner, Rob Nelson, Best Friends Photos (Janet & Lisa), and everyone else who pitched in to help—Thank you. For without your help, I could not have brought The Wraith and his world to life. Without you, I would not have been able to do this film at all. You all were the backbone, workers, inspirations, and friends who helped us achieve such a great film. For the help and support, I bow in honor.

Last but not least...Frank Dirscherl. Frank you took a chance with me when no one else would. No one would see my vision of films and how I thought they should work. People trashed my films for the most part and you saw beyond that and saw someone who understood how The Wraith should be done. You put faith in me and I thank you for that. I thank you for allowing me the opportunity to portray your character and his world on screen through my camera. That took guts, courage, and faith. Thank you. Thank you for everything you've done for me personally and the film. Thanks for listening to me vent and rant and (like a sitcom theme song) thank you for being a friend. You've had my back every step of the way and I appreciate it dearly. I will one day make your Wraith feature film, but until then, I hope this one will suffice. It's been a great ride so far, mate. Let's see how far we can take it!

This is the last Lair Line I'm doing. Production on the film is nearing its end and we're almost ready to premiere the film. Frank will still be posting news and information regarding the film, but this Lair Line section set out to be the production diary to the film, and now it appears production is nearing an end. As the production ends, I feel I should end the Lair Line this way. I'll still frequent Frank's site, but the production chapter of *The Wraith* is now officially closed. Writing this is bittersweet. I feel as though I have revealed so much of myself through these Lair Lines that to stop is almost selfish on my part. However, I know I must stop them now and move on to getting the film out there for you all to see. I will honestly miss writing the Lair Line production diary. I hope over the course of me writing it that everyone has got some insight now into what it's like making a movie at the level we made *The Wraith* at. I hope you've all got to know me better and that I've at least entertained you through these journal entries.

Thank you all for your support. Be sure to check out *The Wraith: Eyes of Judgment* wherever you can, and if I'm there selling or supporting it, stop by and let me know what you think of it. I love talking to people, but most of all, I love talking to people about my movies. Haha.

Thanks to everyone involved in this film, everyone on Frank's website, and every other site that has done any news piece or press release on us. Thank you all for your support and faith in Sir Reel Films. Thanks to my wife and son for their support, and for putting up with my workaholism. I love you all.

See you at the movies.

Ramble On...

Stephen

THE WRAITH
Eyes of Judgment

Photos from the set and film

Captions by

Stephen Semones

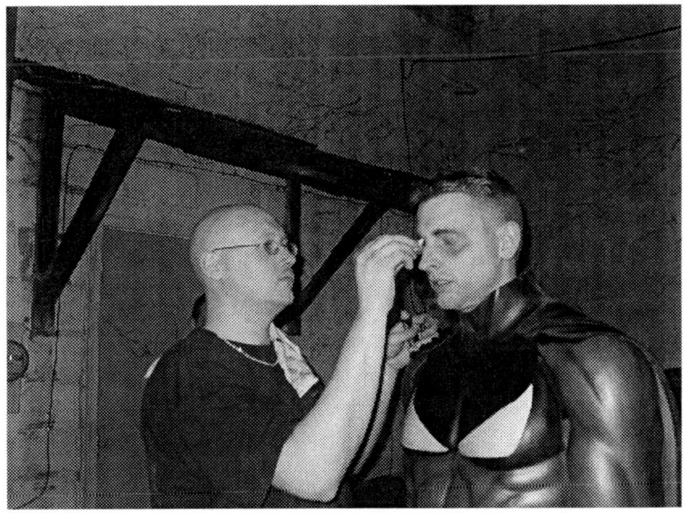

Stephen Semones darkening the eyes of David Cooper just before putting on the mask.

The Wraith (David Cooper) on location just before filming a fight scene.

Robert Latham (Rick McVey)

"The Money Shot" - Leena Patterson expresses how much she loves her superhero in his Lair.

From Left to Right- Randy Stout (Eight Ball), David Cooper (The Wraith), Zek Hensley (Chains), and Mandi Leigh (Emma Madison) just before posing for a cast photo.

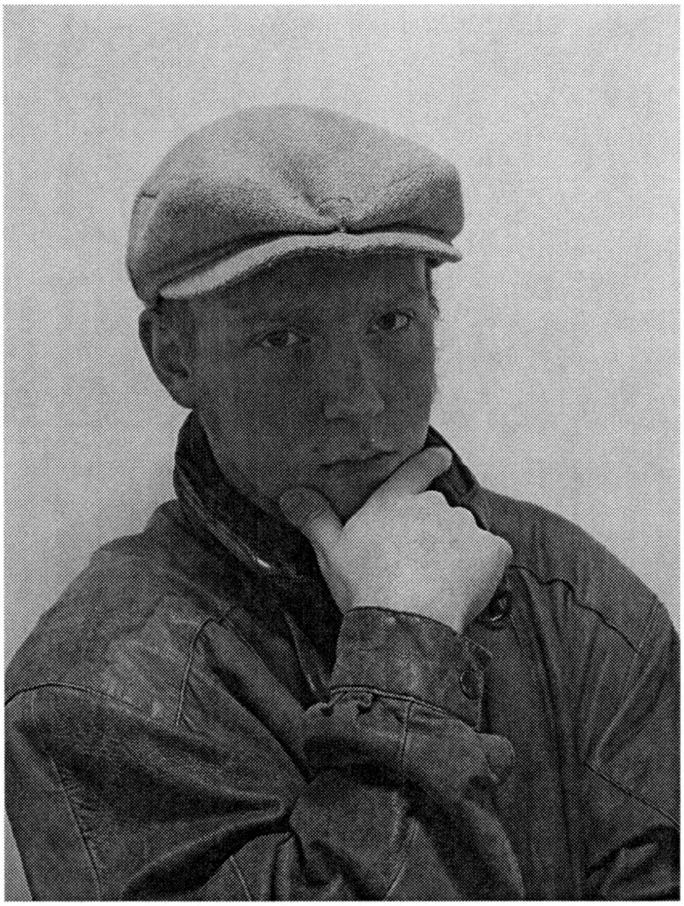

Max Horton (Nathan Blevins), The Wraith's trusted driver.

Eight Ball (Randy Stout) posing in character for a photo.

Cast and crew listen intently as Stephen Semones walks through his vision of the scene.

Stephen Semones directing Mandi Leigh for the Home of Darkness music video shoot. Zek Hensley sitting on the steps helping with lighting.

Early production of the Wraith cowl by Universal Designs.

From left to right, Derik Nutter, Stephen Semones, Zek Hensley setting up equipment just before filming the fight scene involving Mandi Leigh.

Finished Wraith cowl by Universal Designs.

The Wraith posing with Austin Turner, son of stylist Christie Turner, on set just before a fight scene.

Walking through the Wraith Lair (greenscreen shoot) with Stacie Cooper (l), Stephen Semones (middle), Nathan Blevins (cr), and David Cooper (r)

Robert Latham enters his office to find a visitor (The Cobra).

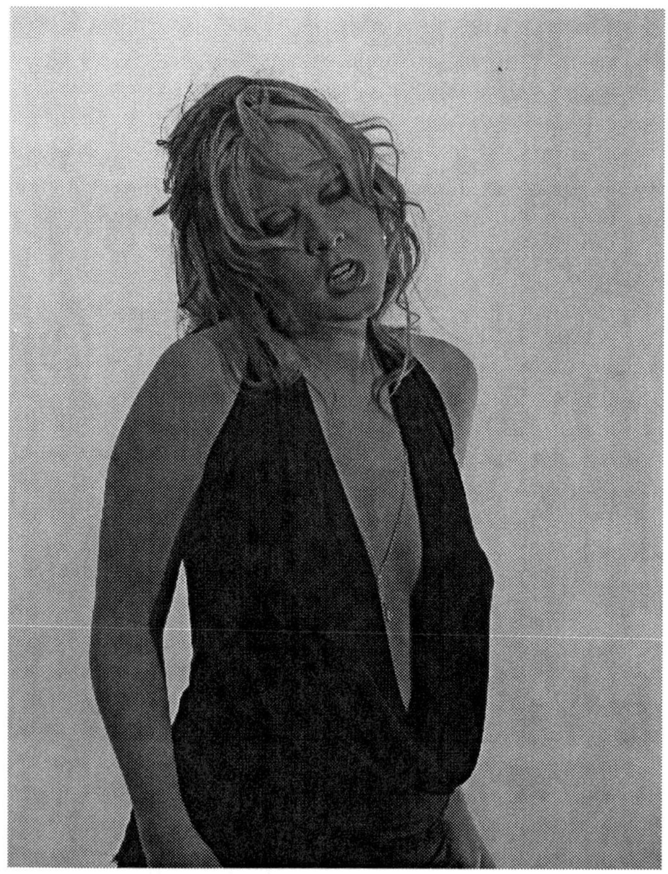

Mandi Leigh in front of a greenscreen during production of the music video, Home of Darkness.

David Cooper just before filming a fight scene, posing for a promo pic.

Stephen Semones directing his brother, David.

Chains (Zek Hensley) is about to slap Emma Madison (Mandi Leigh) as Eight Ball (Randy Stout) holds her down.

Composer Adam DiTroia at work.

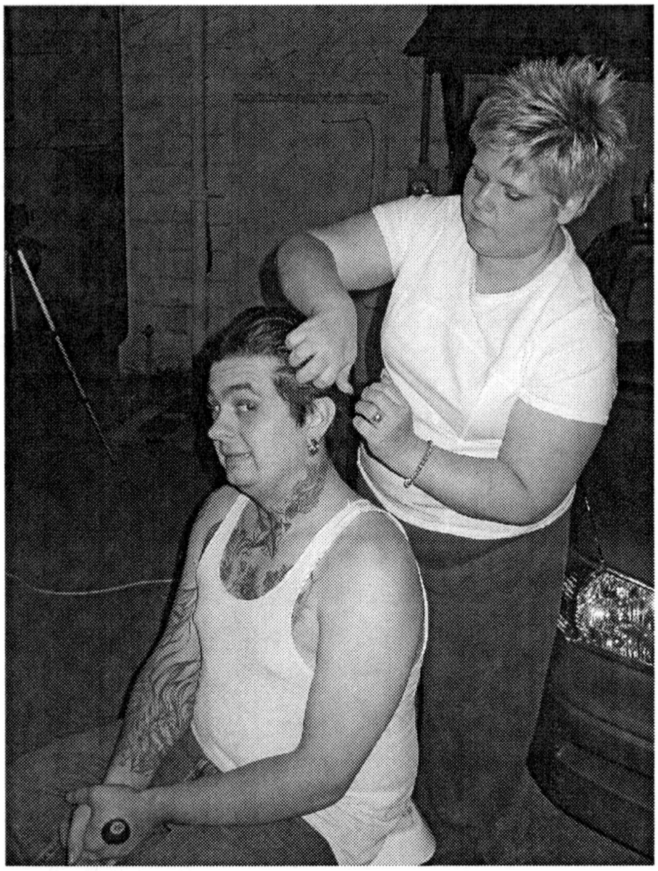

Stylist Christie Turner working on the hair for Eight Ball

Stephen Semones directing/running camera to get a close-up angle on David Cooper as he's about to deliver some serious dialogue. Stacie Cooper watches on as her husband prepares for the scene.

Stacie and David Cooper

Mandi Leigh and David Cooper posing for the camera.

Upward angle of The Wraith
in front of a greenscreen.

David Semones caught off guard with a photo op.

Stephen Semones and Assistant Director Ty Kelsey
lining up a camera angle.

A CGI model for the Wraith Lair.

The Wraith in front of a greenscreen. Later, Metro City was added in by FX wizard, Marc Kimball.

Marc Kimball, Visual FX Supervisor/wizard.

Ryan Basham as The Cobra.

Photo taken in between takes during filming of the opening fight sequence. A quick mean pose for the camera and then David Cooper was off cutting up and having fun in the suit.

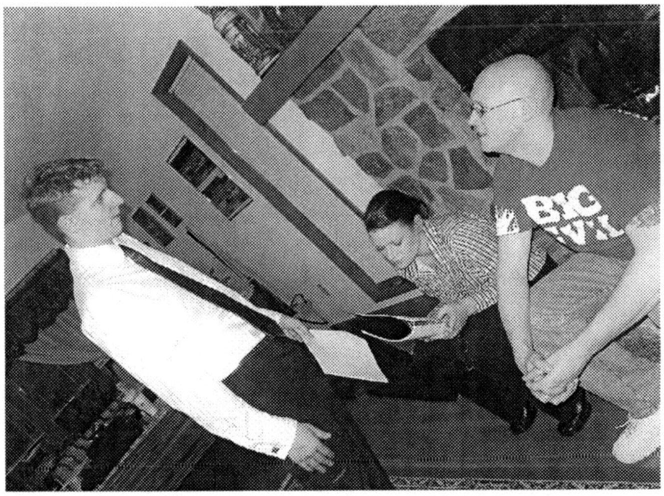

David Cooper, Stacie Cooper, listening to Stephen Semones discuss the dialogue they are about to deliver.

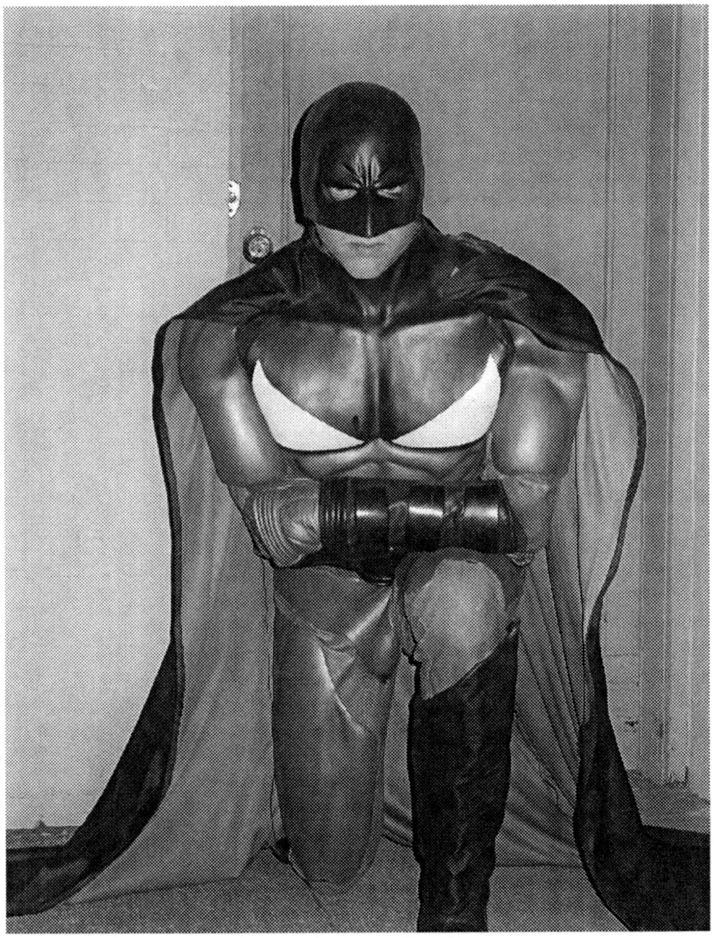

Picture taken on location outside an alley; David Cooper posing for the camera in costume.

David Semones and David Cooper practicing for the final fight sequence of the film.

Emmy Award-winning Composer, Larry Groupé supplied the "Wraith Theme" for the film.

Stephen Semones directing and running camera for an alley scene with The Wraith.

Promo shot of The Wraith.

Close up of The Wraith standing in front of a greenscreen.

Another promo shot.

Charlie Grieco covers his boss's back.

Ty Kelsey (l), David Cooper, Sean Semones and Stephen Semones (r).

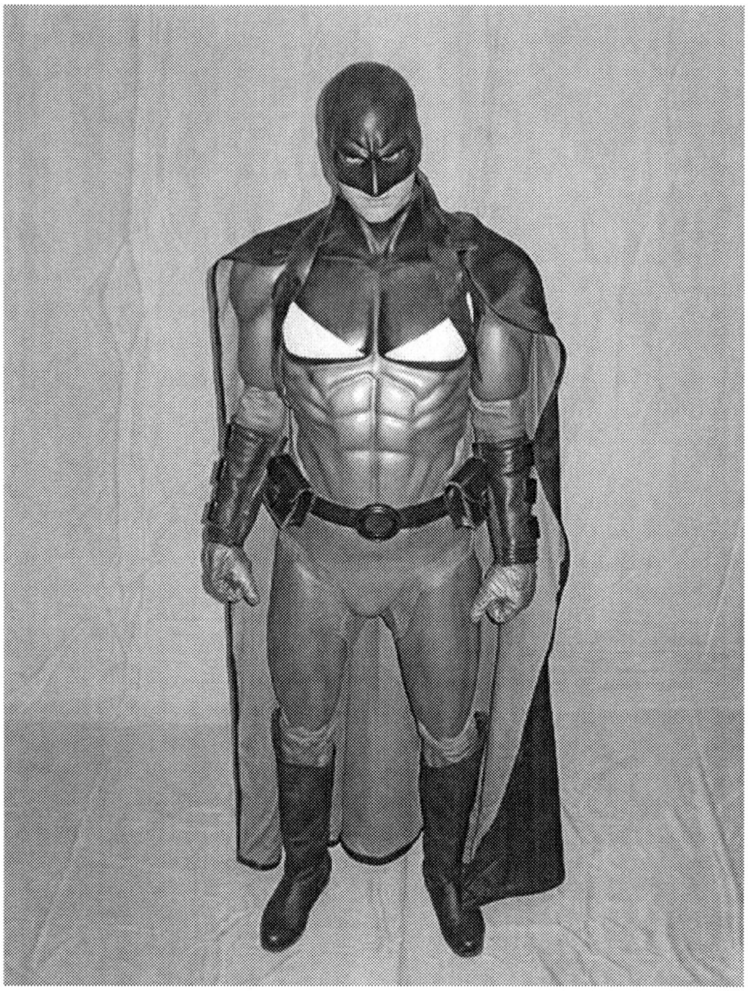

The Wraith in front of a greenscreen.

The Wraith.

Special Wraith comic exclusive! Read on!

THE LEGEND OF THE WRAITH
Who he is and how he came to be
WRITTEN BY
Frank Dirscherl
ILLUSTRATED BY
Eliseu Gouveia
LETTERING BY
Dave Rothe
ONLY A VERY FEW CLOSE TO ME KNOW THIS STORY...
KNOW HOW I BECAME...
THE WRAITH
IN LAYING OUT THIS STORY--
I WANT PEOPLE TO KNOW THE TRUTH.
ONE WAY
I ONCE WAS A COP BY THE NAME OF MICHAEL REEVE.
IDEALISTIC AND HONEST--
--I ALWAYS FOUGHT TO MAKE METRO CITY A BETTER PLACE.
DESPITE HAVING NO FAMILY, I HAD THE LOVE OF A GOOD WOMAN--
LEENA PATTERSON.
BUT OUR RELATIONSHIP WAS GOING NOWHERE...

AFTER ANOTHER NIGHT OF LEENA AND I FAILING TO RESOLVE OUR DIFFERENCES...
MY LIFE CHANGED FOREVER.
HAVING BEEN RIDICULED BY MY POLICE COLLEAGUES FOR BELIEVING IN METRO'S BOGEY-MAN...
...IT'S IRONIC THAT HE CHOSE ME AS HIS REPLACEMENT WHEN HE WAS MORTALLY WOUNDED.
...THROUGH SOME MYSTICAL MEANS STILL UNKNOWN TO ME...
THE WRAITH TRANSFERRED ALL HIS POWERS, HIS MEMORIES, EVERYTHING, INTO ME.
NOW BELIEVING MYSELF TO BE PAUL SANDERSON, THE TRUE WRAITH. I BEGAN MY NEW LIFE, WITH THE HELP OF SANDERSON'S ASSOCIATES--
MAX HORTON AND JONATHAN SIMPSON, UNAWARE OF WHAT I LEFT BEHIND.
BUT SOMETHING WENT WRONG. DESPITE MY LOSS OF MEMORY, I COULDN'T FORGET LEENA, AND THE MEMORY OF MY PREVIOUS LIFE CAME FLOODING BACK.
REALIZING I COULDN'T GO BACK, I TRIED TO EXPLAIN TO LEENA OF MY DECISION TO REMAIN PAUL SANDERSON...
AND THE WRAITH.
BUT LEENA STOOD FIRM, AND REFUSED TO LEAVE ME.
I CAME TO REALIZE MY OWN STRONG FEELINGS... WE FINALLY CAME TO AN UNDERSTANDING, AND OUR RELATIONSHIP BECAME ALL THE STRONGER FOR IT.
NOW WE STAND TOGETHER, A TEAM FORGED OF NEW AND OLD, OF LOVE AND HONOR.
NOW I AM, FOREVER MORE,
THE WRAITH!

TAYLOR & JEFF '03
THE
WRAITH
www.the-wraith.com

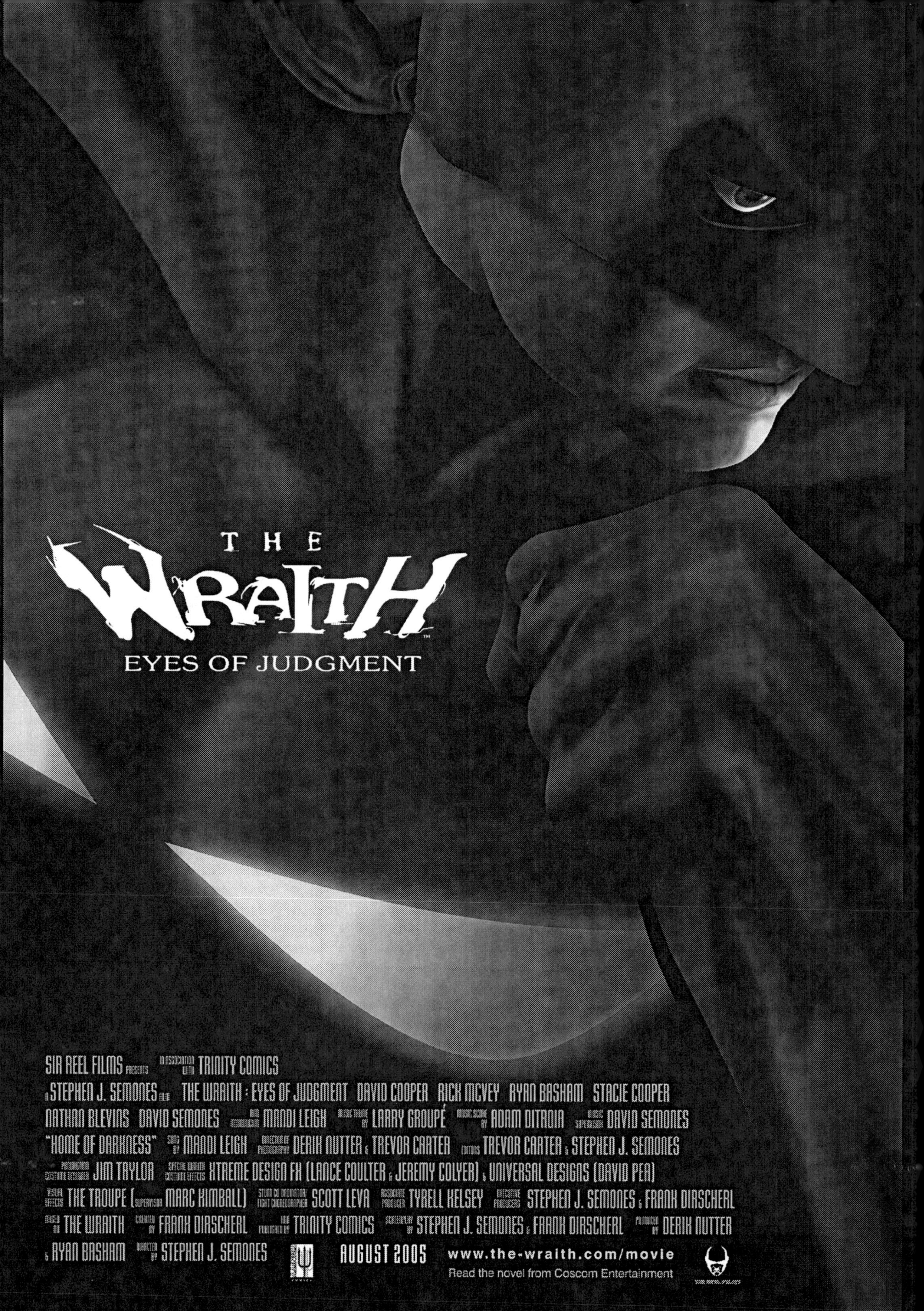
THE WRAITH
EYES OF JUDGMENT
SIR REEL FILMS TRINITY COMICS
STEPHEN J. SEMONES THE WRAITH : EYES OF JUDGMENT DAVID COOPER RICK MCVEY RYAN BASHAM STACIE COOPER
NATHAN BLEVINS DAVID SEMONES MANDI LEIGH LARRY GROUPÉ ADAM DITROIA DAVID SEMONES
"HOME OF DARKNESS" MANDI LEIGH DERIK NUTTER & TREVOR CARTER TREVOR CARTER & STEPHEN J. SEMONES
JIM TAYLOR XTREME DESIGN FX (LANCE COULTER & JEREMY COLYER) & UNIVERSAL DESIGNS (DAVID PEA)
THE TROUPE (MARC KIMBALL) SCOTT LEVA TYRELL KELSEY STEPHEN J. SEMONES & FRANK DIRSCHERL
THE WRAITH FRANK DIRSCHERL TRINITY COMICS STEPHEN J. SEMONES & FRANK DIRSCHERL DERIK NUTTER
& RYAN BASHAM STEPHEN J. SEMONES
AUGUST 2005
www.the-wraith.com/movie
Read the novel from Coscom Entertainment

Printed in the United States
83040LV00007B/1/A